THE
JOURNEY

Exodus

NELSON
IMPACT™
Bible Study Series

THE
JOURNEY

Exodus

NELSON IMPACT
A Division of Thomas Nelson Publishers
Since 1798

www.thomasnelson.com

The publishers are grateful to Michael Christopher for his collaboration, writing skills, and editorial help in developing the content for this book.

Published by Nelson Impact, a Division of Thomas Nelson, Inc., P.O. Box 141000, Nashville, Tennessee 37214.

ISBN 1-4185-0616-8

Printed in the United States of America.

06 07 08 EB 9 8 7 6 5 4 3 2 1

A Word from the Publisher…

*Be diligent to present yourself approved to God, a worker who does not need
to be ashamed, rightly dividing the word of truth.*

2 Timothy 2:15 NKJV

We are so glad that you have chosen this study guide to enrich your biblical knowledge and strengthen your walk with God. Inside you will find great information that will deepen your understanding and knowledge of this book of the Bible.

Many tools are included to aid you in your study, including ancient and present-day maps of the Middle East, as well as timelines and charts to help you understand when the book was written and why. You will also benefit from sidebars placed strategically throughout this study guide, designed to give you expanded knowledge of language, theology, culture, and other details regarding the Scripture being studied.

We consider it a joy and a ministry to serve you and teach you through these study guides. May your heart be blessed, your mind expanded, and your spirit lifted as you walk through God's Word.

Blessings,

Edward (Les) Middleton, M.Div.
Editor-in-Chief, Nelson Impact

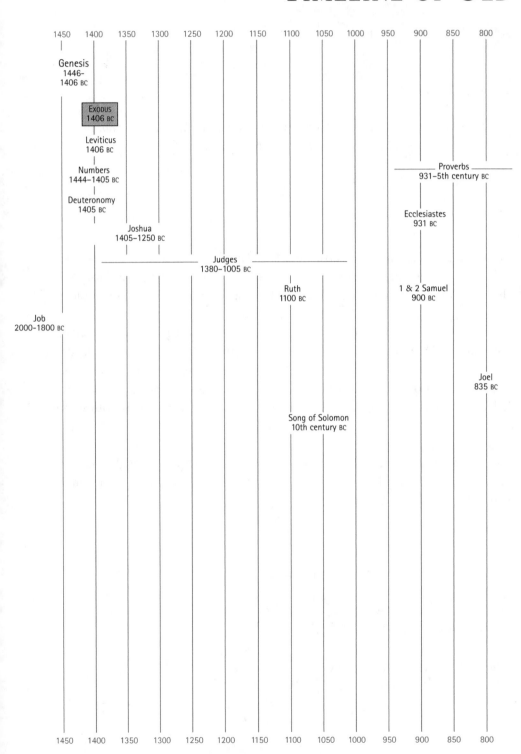

Testament Writings

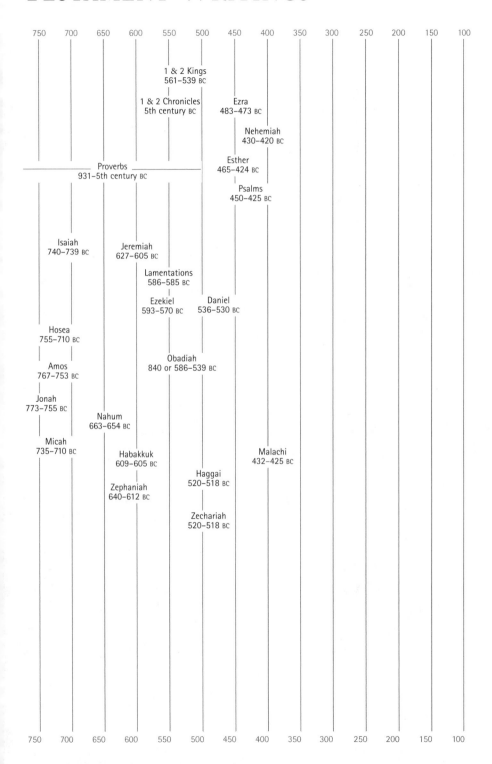

| | 750 | 700 | 650 | 600 | 550 | 500 | 450 | 400 | 350 | 300 | 250 | 200 | 150 | 100 |

1 & 2 Kings
561–539 BC

1 & 2 Chronicles
5th century BC

Ezra
483–473 BC

Nehemiah
430–420 BC

Esther
465–424 BC

Proverbs
931–5th century BC

Psalms
450–425 BC

Isaiah
740–739 BC

Jeremiah
627–605 BC

Lamentations
586–585 BC

Ezekiel
593–570 BC

Daniel
536–530 BC

Hosea
755–710 BC

Amos
767–753 BC

Obadiah
840 or 586–539 BC

Jonah
773–755 BC

Nahum
663–654 BC

Micah
735–710 BC

Malachi
432–425 BC

Habakkuk
609–605 BC

Haggai
520–518 BC

Zephaniah
640–612 BC

Zechariah
520–518 BC

| | 750 | 700 | 650 | 600 | 550 | 500 | 450 | 400 | 350 | 300 | 250 | 200 | 150 | 100 |

OLD MIDDLE EAST

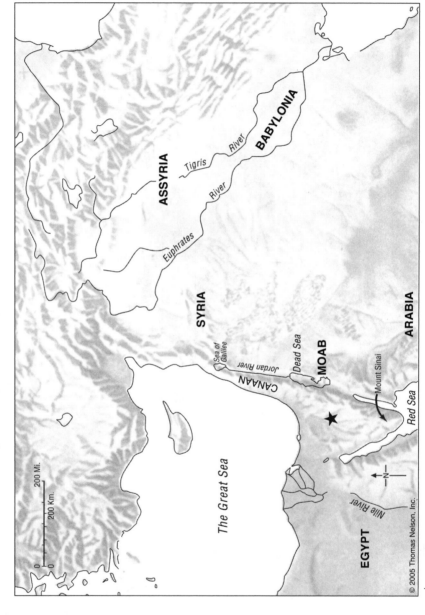

★ The book of Exodus was written in the wilderness south of Canaan.

© 2005 Thomas Nelson, Inc.

MIDDLE EAST OF TODAY

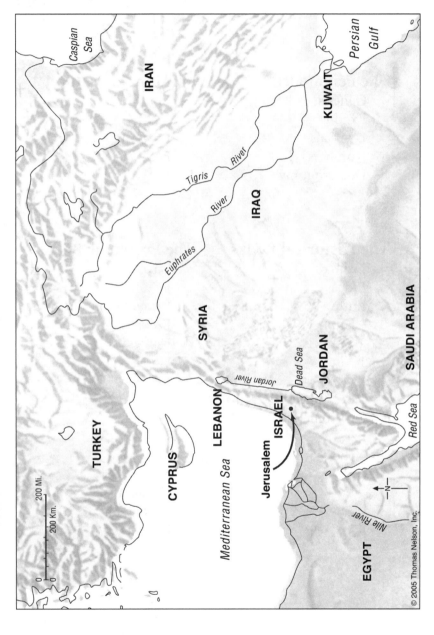

OLD TESTAMENT DIVISIONS

The Pentateuch
Genesis
Exodus
Leviticus
Numbers
Deuteronomy

Wisdom Literature
Job
Psalms
Proverbs
Ecclesiastes
Song of Solomon

The Historical Books
Joshua
Judges
Ruth
1 Samuel
2 Samuel
1 Kings
2 Kings
1 Chronicles
2 Chronicles
Ezra
Nehemiah
Esther

The Prophetic Books
Isaiah
Jeremiah
Lamentations
Ezekiel
Daniel
Hosea
Joel
Amos
Obadiah
Jonah
Micah
Nahum
Habakkuk
Zephaniah
Haggai
Zechariah
Malachi

New Testament Divisions

The Four Gospels
Matthew
Mark
Luke
John

History
Acts

The Epistles of Paul
Romans
1 Corinthians
2 Corinthians
Galatians
Ephesians
Philippians
Colossians
1 Thessalonians
2 Thessalonians
1 Timothy
2 Timothy
Titus
Philemon

The General Epistles
Hebrews
James
1 Peter
2 Peter
1 John
2 John
3 John
Jude

Apocalyptic Literature
Revelation

ICON KEY

Throughout this study guide, you will find many icon sidebars that will aid and enrich your study of this book of the Bible. To help you identify what these icons represent, please refer to the key below.

BIBLICAL GRAB BAG

A biblical grab bag full of interesting facts and tidbits.

BIBLE

Further exploration of biblical principles and interpretations, along with a little food for thought.

LANGUAGE

Word usages, definitions, interpretations, and information on the Greek and Hebrew languages.

CULTURE

Customs, traditions, and lifestyle practices in biblical times.

ARCHAEOLOGICAL

Archaeological discoveries and artifacts that relate to biblical life, as well as modern-day discoveries.

CONTENTS

INTRODUCTION

The book of Exodus is unique in several fascinating ways. For example, in terms of its historical scope and theological significance, the subject matter of Exodus is much "grander" than that of almost any other book of the Bible.

Nowhere else, it could be argued, does God interact in such a "grand" way with His own people—especially with Moses. Nowhere else does God do such grand things to preserve and protect His own. Nowhere else does God give us such a grand portrait of Himself (Exod. 34:6–7). And nowhere else does God give the children of Israel—and through them, the entire world—such an awe-inspiring view of right and wrong as He does in the Ten Commandments.

Furthermore, leaving theological and moral/ethical matters aside for the moment, the events in the book of Exodus have served as the inspiration for a number of artistic expressions down through the centuries. Exodus-based works of art include countless paintings, books, musical scores, plays, and even works combining more than one medium in one vehicle. Thus Gioacchino Rossini (perhaps most widely known for the unforgettable theme music of *The Lone Ranger* via the "William Tell Overture") united music and drama in a brilliant opera called *Mosè*. In true operatic fashion, it told the story of the crossing of the Red Sea, but then added a bogus love story between Pharaoh's son and Moses' niece!

Perhaps a more familiar example would be the 1956 Cecil B. DeMille Technicolor epic called *The Ten Commandments,* in which Charlton Heston attained permanent "voice of God" status, playing both God and Moses at the same time. Whether this particular movie is truly "art" is a different question—certainly it was suitably grand. But more important, it was entirely inspired by the book of Exodus.

WHY IS THE BIBLE SO "ARTISTIC"?

Why has God's Word inspired so much art over the last several thousand years? And by art we don't just mean paintings—although it's possible that more Western-world paintings have been based on biblical subject matter than on any other source. The word *art* also encompasses books, plays, music, sculptures, and even movies.

The answer is simple. No other book is so near-universal in its appeal, its popularity, or its distribution within almost any given population. More important, no other book is so worthy of the "grand" treatment of art yet simultaneously so acceptable at all levels of society—with, sadly, the possible exception of any government-supported facility in the modern United States.

THE GOING OUT

The original Hebrew name for the book of Exodus is typically transliterated *W'elleh sh'mot,* meaning "these are the names." More commonly, in modern Hebrew it is simply called *Sh'mot,* meaning "names." Both of these designations derive from the very first verse, which begins, "Now these are the names of the children of Israel who came to Egypt" (Exod. 1:1 NKJV).

The English name Exodus is basically a transliteration of the Greek name for this book, which was first used to refer to it in the Septuagint, the earliest Greek translation of the Old Testament Scriptures prepared in Alexandria between 300 and 200 BC. *Exodus* means "a going out," which is an obvious reference to the main event of Exodus, the "going out" of the children of Israel from bondage in Egypt.

MOSES, THE AUTHOR

The question of Moses' authorship is not so easily settled, at least among certain scholars. Some of them start with the assumption that Moses could not have written the book of Exodus, then analyze it from a number of different viewpoints and attempt thereby to prove their original hypothesis. Others claim that the basic text of Exodus came from oral history and was passed down through the generations for several centuries before someone finally wrote it all down.

Yet the Bible specifically offers its own internal proof that Moses was, indeed, the inspired author of Exodus. Consider the following list of verses from Exodus and Deuteronomy, which is by no means a complete listing of every reference to Moses' authorship in the Bible, but rather will give you a fair sampling:

> The LORD said to Moses, "Write this for a memorial in the book and recount it in the hearing of Joshua." (Exod. 17:14 NKJV)

> Moses wrote all the words of the LORD. And he rose early in the morning, and built an altar at the foot of the mountain, and twelve pillars according to the twelve tribes of Israel. (Exod. 24:4 NKJV)

> He was there with the LORD forty days and forty nights; he neither ate bread nor drank water. And He wrote on the tablets the words of the covenant, the Ten Commandments. (Exod. 34:28 NKJV)

> Moses wrote this law and delivered it to the priests, the sons of Levi, who bore the ark of the covenant of the LORD, and to all the elders of Israel. (Deut. 31:9 NKJV)

> So it was, when Moses had completed writing the words of this law in a book. . . . (Deut. 31:24 NKJV)

In addition, we are told in Acts 7:22 that "Moses was learned in all the wisdom of the Egyptians" (NKJV), thus settling the question of whether Moses had the requisite training and education he would have needed. Beyond that, in Mark 7:10 Jesus Himself used the words "Moses said" to introduce quotations from Exodus. A few chapters later, He also said, "Have you not read in the book of Moses, in the burning bush passage, how God spoke to him, saying, 'I am the God of Abraham, the God of Isaac, and the God of Jacob'?" (Mark 12:26 NKJV).

Finally, despite the incredible accuracy with which the ancient Jews were able to transmit various oral documents down through history (e.g., the Mishnah, or "oral commentary," dates back thousands of years but was not written down until the second or third century AD), it still seems inconceivable that God would allow something as important as the Ten Commandments—His very own words—to be recorded for all the millions of people God knew would come after, by a system that depended on the cumulative memories of hundreds of people who were not there, did not hear the voice of God, and had no firsthand knowledge whatsoever of what He had to say.

WITHIN MOSES' LIFETIME

For those who accept the Bible's own word on the authorship issue, the same quotations (and several more that we have not included here) answer the remaining question of *when* the book of Exodus was written. Obviously it was written during Moses' lifetime, most likely during those times when the children of Israel were not, literally, on the march.

And when did the Exodus come about? Well, contrary to the movie version mentioned above, which positions the Exodus from Egypt during the reign of Ramses II in the thirteenth century BC, most scholars agree that it probably occurred somewhere near the middle of the fifteenth century BC. Their reasons fall into three general categories, each one illustrated below by just one example among dozens that could be cited.

1. *The biblical record.* First Kings 6:1 tells us that King Solomon began to build his temple in the fourth year of his reign, which occurred "in the four hundred and eightieth year after the children of Israel had come out of the land of Egypt" (NKJV). The fourth year of Solomon's reign was 966 BC, which would put the Exodus in 1446 BC.

2. *Archeological evidence at the source.* Thutmose IV became pharaoh of Egypt after his father, Amenhotep II—but he was not the oldest son—because the oldest son of Amenhotep was killed by the angel of death on the night of the first Passover. Amenhotep II was involved in a number of massive building projects in northern Egypt that are generally dated to the 1567–1379 BC time period. During this same period we know that members of Semitic tribes (which included those who were later called Jews) were forced to make bricks for Egyptian construction projects.

3. *Archeological evidence at the destination.* The record of events in Palestine, which is where the Jews ended up, suggests that several cities were destroyed around 1400 BC, including Jericho, Ai, and Hazor, all of which were destroyed by Joshua and his army as recorded in the book of Joshua.

WHO SAYS MOSES WAS SO HUMBLE?

One of the more fascinating aspects of the Bible, from a cultural/ sociological/linguistic perspective, is what some scholars have called the "pattern of interchange" between God and His people—especially between God and Moses. Others have called it the "Jewish-mother" syndrome, which is not meant in a negative sense whatsoever—it's just a matter of how some of those interchanges were structured.

Think of this as you read through the book of Exodus and respond to the study material in the chapters ahead. Rather than trying right now to deal with specific examples, just watch for them—and enjoy them—as they come up! For example, many times a typical God-Moses interchange will begin with a question that alludes to the subject about to be discussed but doesn't exactly identify it in clear, unambiguous terms. Indeed, sometimes the question will be downright oblique. For example, Moses might say, "What am I? What is my sin that You should treat me like this? Do You wish me dead? Wouldn't it be easier just to kill me?"

Or, as God actually does say in at least one place, "What? Is My right arm suddenly too short? Do I not have the same power I had yesterday?" In other words, "Why in the world are you doubting Me now, when I've never failed you before?"

What seems especially ironic about the above is that both God and Moses focused on the same thing—God's own sufficiency in every conceivable situation. About this very thing, God often *reminded* and Moses always *acknowledged*. Undoubtedly this is what kept Moses in his position as God's direct emissary to His people. And to some extent this also explains why Moses was considered the most humble of all God's people, and thus the greatest of all the children of Israel. To be humble in the presence of God is to get completely over the idea that you have any personal control over whatever's going on. God was completely in charge, and Moses always knew it. Therefore, Moses' arguments often had to do with the "why" aspect of a given situation, but seldom with the "what" or even the "how."

Indeed, when Moses asked why, he was often just trying to understand God better so that he could be in closer accord with Him. He was really asking to be heard, "venting" in a way that kept the focus on God and what God was trying to achieve rather than on Moses himself. For most people, everything is all about them. For Moses, it was always about God.

The one exception, of course, was the time when God finally told Moses to be quiet and not bring up a particular subject again. But we won't tell you about that here, for it happened in the book of Deuteronomy, which surely you will encounter later on.

WHO CAN FATHOM . . .

Many people find tremendous comfort in the very first verse of Exodus, for it ties in directly to what Jesus Himself said of the Good Shepherd in John 10:3: "He calls his own sheep by name and leads them out" (NKJV). God, through Moses, did exactly the same thing at the beginning of Exodus. That is, He identified *by name* the eleven sons of Jacob who came down with Jacob into Egypt at the invitation of Jacob's other son, Joseph, and with the express permission of Pharaoh. Truly God *is* the Good Shepherd.

DELIVERANCE AND WORSHIP

It would be almost impossible to sum up the entire story of Exodus in one word, but if we absolutely had no choice, we could do a reasonably good job of it in two words: *deliverance* and *worship*. With respect to the former, on a human scale, Exodus tells us the fascinating, uplifting story of God's physical deliverance of His people from their centuries-long bondage in Egypt. But on a much larger, spiritual scale, Exodus tells us how God made possible the deliverance from sin of all humankind.

He began with the ancient children of Israel by honoring His original covenant with Abraham, Isaac, and Jacob and delivering their descendants from physical bondage. He then established the back-and-forth nature of that covenant by explaining, through Moses, what humankind's reciprocal responsibilities would include. And we use the word *humankind* on purpose, for even though the children of Israel were set apart (i.e., sanctified) as God's chosen people, He soon extended the same invitation to anyone else who might desire to sojourn among them and thus be treated as equals among His chosen ones.

In other words, roughly the first eighteen chapters of Exodus detail God's deliverance of His people; the remaining twenty-two chapters explain how they were to worship Him. "You shall not murder," "You shall not steal," and all the rest are nothing more and nothing less than the basic standards of behavior that God requires all of us to observe in return for His approval and blessing.

Beyond that, He also wants us to establish personal relationships with Him—relationships that cannot be had by someone else on our behalf. But these are doctrinal matters and are beyond the scope of this study guide. Let us concentrate instead on what some have called the official "forming of a nation" as described by Moses.

That the children of Israel were intended by God to be a holy nation is beyond dispute. That they wound up wavering, stumbling, and "taking another lap around the mountain" more than once is also beyond dispute. But none of their failures made God love them any less, and none of their failures made Him strive any less to bring redemption to them whether they deserved it or not.

And so it is with us.

OPPRESSION

EXODUS 1:1–22

Before We Begin . . .

Can you briefly recount the story of how Jacob and all his descendants came to be in Egypt in the first place? How did they get there? Why? What series of events served as the major catalyst that brought them down from Canaan?

Given Joseph's immense popularity (and his life-and-death value!) to the Egyptian pharaoh during his lifetime, does it not seem reasonable to expect that the Egyptian kings who came to power later on would still act kindly toward Joseph's family? If not, why not?

Chapter 1 of Exodus provides a short transition between the end of Genesis and the main events of Exodus, linking all that had gone before with what was about to happen. The book of Genesis ended with the death of Joseph, in Egypt, surrounded by his surviving brothers, their wives, and their children. Joseph's brothers—the other eleven sons of Jacob—are listed in verses 2–4, with verse 5 noting that "Joseph was in Egypt already" when his brothers came down to Egypt from Canaan with their father.

Exodus picks up the story approximately four hundred years later, by which time God has seen fit to multiply the descendants of Jacob (who was also called Israel) and make them a huge nation of perhaps two million people, exactly as He had promised Abraham many years before. But things have not gone well for the children of Israel since the deaths of Joseph and the pharaoh (i.e., the Egyptian king) he served so admirably during times of famine and uncertainty. Indeed—when Exodus opens, the current king of Egypt (most likely Amenhotep II) does not even remember Joseph. Most assuredly, he does not believe that the nation he now commands owes any kind of a perpetual debt to the members of Joseph's family.

But before we get ahead of ourselves, please read the first seven verses of chapter 1 and answer the following questions.

Exodus 1

Israel's Suffering in Egypt

What were the names of the children of Israel who came to Egypt, as told in verses 2–4? REUBEN, SIMEON, LEVI AND JUDAH; ISSACHAR, ZEBULUN AND BENJAMAN; DAN, NAPHTALI, GAD AND ASHER

What was the family relationship of these men? SONS THEY WERE

In total, how many descendants of Jacob came down to Egypt with him? 70

Verse 6 tells us that Joseph and his brothers and "all that generation" (meaning wives, cousins, etc.) eventually died. Based on what you already know of this story, why would this fact be significant? HERE iT REFERS to ALL OF A PARTiCULAR CLASS LiViNG At A dESiGNATEd tiME.

BRICKS FROM THE RIVER

When the Israelites were slaves of the Egyptians, they were forced to make huge numbers of bricks—as we will see in subsequent chapters of Exodus. The process was really quite simple but involved a lot of dirty, backbreaking work. If you have ever seen the movie *The Ten Commandments,* you know exactly what we mean!

Workers packed a mixture of Nile River mud and straw into wooden molds. The straw acted as a reinforcing agent, much as metal rebar (and sometimes steel netting) is used to reinforce modern construction concrete. The mud bricks were left to dry in the sun and were used as cheap building materials.

Nonetheless, did the children of Israel dwindle in terms of numbers, or did they continue to multiply? they were fruitful and increased greatly.

Do you think the answer to the above question would represent a blessing or a curse from God? Why would God be interested in how many descendants Jacob might have? A blessing they became exceedingly mighty so the land was filled with them

Verses 8 and 9 introduce us to the pharaoh of Moses' time, a man who obviously had the welfare of his own people close to his heart. He also had certain concerns about the children of Israel as well, but they were not concerns about *their* welfare!

Why did the new king seem to be afraid of the children of Israel (vv. 8–10)? What was the "worst case" he imagined? they were out numbered and mightier

What was the relationship between the hard work and physical hardships Pharaoh inflicted upon Israel and Israel's own growth rate (v. 12)? Do you see any irony here? tHE MORE tHEY WERE Afflicted tHE MORE tHEY MULtiplized ANd speAd out.

What did Pharaoh instruct the Hebrew midwives to do (vv. 15–16)?

MIDWIVES AND BIRTHING STOOLS

From ancient times, midwives have been the indispensable assistants at literally millions and millions of non-hospital births. The ancient Hebrew midwives were no different from most others in any important respects. In fact, both the children of Israel and the Egyptians used birthing stools, sometimes owned by the midwives, who carried them with them from one birth to the next. Typically this would be a low stool, shaped like a horseshoe, with a fixed shelf located slightly below the level of the curved seat, on which a pillow or other soft material could be placed.

On the other hand, some scholars believe that Hebrew midwives did not always use actual birthing stools—that, instead, the Hebrew women simply sat on two adjoining stones to get the same result. Either way, when the time was right, the mother-to-be sat on the rim of the stool (or on the edges of the two stones) with her legs pulled up so that she could literally deliver the baby directly onto a pillow. The midwife would coordinate the efforts of other women if the mother needed help supporting herself on the stool, and she would help in any other way she could. But mostly she was there to assure the mother that all was going well. And then, of course, to swaddle the baby in soft bandages and gently deliver the baby to the mother's arms.

Incidentally, although Exodus 1:15 lists only two Hebrew midwives, given the size of the Hebrew population they served, these two were undoubtedly responsible for organizing and supervising a much larger group of midwives who handled the actual birth-assistance duties.

Did they obey him? Why or why not?

How did God respond to what the midwives did?

What was Pharaoh's command to his people (v. 22)?

Thus the stage is now set for the birth of Moses and for the mighty hand of God to come sweeping down onto Egypt, bringing His people out from bondage, and making them into a great nation through which He could then reveal Himself to all humankind.

Pulling It All Together . . .

- Jacob and all of his sons except Joseph came down together to Egypt from Canaan. Joseph was already there.

- After Joseph died, the new king of Egypt did not know of his legacy and thus began to resent and even fear the children of Israel.

- He made slaves of them, abused them physically, and forced them to build his cities and work in his fields.

- Despite all this, the Israelite population continued to grow. So Pharaoh commanded the Hebrew midwives to kill all male babies as soon as they were born.

- But even this tactic did not work. So Pharaoh commanded his own people to throw male Hebrew babies into the river wherever they found them.

THE DELIVERER

EXODUS 2:1–4:31

Before We Begin ...

The story of the infant Moses, floating in a basket of reeds in the Nile River, is familiar to almost everyone. Assuming that you have heard it before, do you remember how old you were when it was first told to you? Who told you about it? Or did you "hear" it the first time by reading it for yourself?

3rd grade church

What do you already know about the story of the burning bush? Do you believe it's possible that a bush could burn without being destroyed? Why or why not?

YES it was God's will

Why do you believe God calls certain people to do certain jobs? What kind of person would you expect Him to "commission" to lead His own people out of bondage in Egypt?
It's his call. One who would listen to his calling

EXODUS 2

THE BIRTH OF MOSES

This chapter begins with the well-known story of Moses' birth. Chances are you're familiar with most of it already, but let's review the facts, found in the first ten verses, to make sure we're not missing anything important.

Of what "house" (i.e., tribe) were the man and his wife referred to in verse 1? Why do you think their child's ancestry might be significant later on? LEVI

Why did the mother feel the need to hide her son? BECAUSE HE WAS BEAUTIFUL

Where did the mother leave her child when she felt she could no longer hide him at home? IN THE REED BY THE BANK OF THE NILE RIVER

(Note: You might think about your above answer and then ask yourself whether the mother was actually obeying Pharaoh's order to put all male Hebrew babies in the river. Surely the king would not have agreed with her method, but in one sense she was doing exactly as he had commanded.)

Who was watching (and probably helping, as well) as the mother hid the child (v. 4)? MOSES SISTER

Whose daughter found the baby along the riverside (v. 5)? Do you think the mother had something like this in mind? Is it possible she could have chosen that location on purpose, for that very reason? Pharaoh Daughter

Did the woman who found the child know to whom he belonged? YES

Explain your answer.

Who approached Pharaoh's daughter to suggest that a Hebrew woman could nurse the child (v. 7)? We are not given the name of this young girl, but do you know, by name, who she almost certainly was? (If not, the answer will come up later on.)

MOSES SISTER

Verses 8 and 9 contain an incredible irony—one of those frequent examples of God's sense of humor, His sense of justice, and His infinite ability to preserve and protect His own, for His own purposes, all rolled into one. How would you describe that delightful irony?

What name did Pharaoh's daughter give the baby (v. 10)?

What did that name mean?

MOSES FLEES TO MIDIAN

A few years later, when Moses had become a grown man, along came another of those seminal events in his life. It was an event that might have seemed catastrophic at first, yet it was undoubtedly orchestrated by God. Just as Joseph was sent down into Egypt as a slave to prepare and position him for saving his own people when the time came, so Moses was removed from daily life among the Egyptians in order that God could prepare him to be the eventual leader of his own people.

This seems to be God's repeated pattern, for time after time He uses a two-step process in which He first separates, or isolates, various elements (or people) from each other, then develops them into what He desires them to be.

How do you think Moses might have turned out if he'd been allowed to stay with his Egyptian family?

How do you think Moses' sympathies toward his own people might have developed (or not developed)?

Moses definitely knew where he came from, but how do you think he might have changed if he'd led the privileged life of an adopted son, with the Egyptian king as his adoptive grandfather?

Obviously we'll never know, for God clearly had something else in mind. Please read the remainder of chapter 2 of Exodus and answer the following questions to see more of what happened during the early part of Moses' life.

Whom did Moses see beating a Hebrew (v. 11)?

THE COURSE OF DIVINE DEVELOPMENT

One of the things we know about God is that He is a God of order. Nowhere is this more evident than in the way He *creates new things,* whether those things are physical parts of the universe or refashioned people, with their hearts and minds refreshed and prepared for entirely new purposes.

The pattern so often seems to be the same. First comes *separation* of things that God has already created into isolated parts; then comes *development* of those parts into something new and useful to God. The first obvious example involves the universe itself. God separated light from darkness, the heavens from the earth beneath, and the waters from the dry land. Then He developed the sun and the moon, the stars and the planets, the oceans and the continents.

He followed the same pattern when He developed people, beginning with Abraham. First He separated Abram from his own people and his own land; then He tested and developed him; then He entered into permanent covenant with Abraham and promised to make him into a great nation. He did the same with Isaac when He sent him to the land of Haran; with Joseph when He sent him into Egypt; with the Israelites when He brought them out from Egypt, separated them unto themselves in the wilderness, and formed them into a distinct nation unlike any other on earth. Likewise, many years later He sent His own Son into the wilderness for forty days of temptation to develop His persona and help prepare Him for what lay ahead.

Likewise it was with Moses, during the forty years he spent in Midian, separated from his people, while God prepared him for the assignment that only God Himself knew would be coming up. The pattern is clear—and thus the process by which Moses became the great leader of the new nation of Israel was no accident at all, but part of a carefully orchestrated divine plan.

What did Moses do to that person?

What happened next to make Moses fear for his life (vv. 13–15)?

To where did Moses flee to escape Pharaoh's anger?

When he arrived in the land of Midian, Moses sat down at a well, presumably to rest and refresh himself. Before long he was visited by the seven daughters of the local priest who had come to water their flocks. What did Moses do to assist those daughters (v. 17)?

Because Moses helped his daughters, how did the priest repay Moses? Though the Scriptures do not tell us, to what extent do you think that what the priest of Midian did was a common practice in Moses' time?

Moses then began to live with Reuel (the priest) and his daughters. In time, whom did Moses marry (v. 21)?

What did Moses name his son when he was born—and what did that name mean (v. 22)?

Chapter 2 of Exodus concludes with the death of the king of Egypt (probably Thutmose III, who preceded Amenhotep II), but it also adds two or three other very significant pieces of information. For example . . .

What impact did the king's death seem to have on the children of Israel? Were their lives made easier or harder by the new pharaoh who succeeded him?

Obviously God was looking down on what was happening. What was His reaction?

And what, to review once again, was the relationship between God and the children of Israel, with respect to His covenant with Abraham, Isaac, and Jacob?

Given all the above, how would you interpret the word "acknow-ledge" in verse 25: "And God looked upon the children of Israel, and God acknowledged them" (NKJV)? What do you think that word means, beyond simply "taking note of" them?

EXODUS 3

MOSES AT THE BURNING BUSH

Verse 1 of this chapter identifies Moses' father-in-law as Jethro, the name by which he is more commonly known. It is unclear why he was also called Reuel in chapter 2, but apparently he changed his name. Some scholars have suggested that this might have had something to do with the marriage of his daughter Zipporah to Moses, who had been raised within the Egyptian royal family. Perhaps Jethro felt that Moses' background brought him added prestige as well, and thus the change to a name meaning "abundance."

Verse 1 also mentions the "mountain of God." It is no coincidence that this was the same mountain on which Moses later received the Ten Commandments, for Mount Horeb is another name for Mount Sinai.

Now begins a new phase in Moses' life, for God is about to call him into lifelong service.

What did Moses see in the burning bush (v. 2)?

Did the fire consume the bush? In your opinion, why or why not?

Whose voice did Moses hear from the burning bush?

Why was Moses instructed to take off his sandals (v. 5)?

In your own words, according to verses 7–10, why did God contact Moses?

Was Moses confident that he could do the job God asked of him (v. 11)?

What sign did God reference (v. 12)?

Read verses 13–15 and fill in the blanks to see what God told Moses with respect to God's own identity.

> *Then Moses said to God, "Indeed, when I come to the* _____ *of* _____ *and say to them, 'The God of your* _____ *has sent me to you,' and they say to me, 'What is His* _____*?' what shall I say to them?" And* _____ *said to Moses,*
> *"* _____ _____ _____ _____
> _____*." And He said, "Thus you shall say to the* _____ *of* _____*,* ' _____
> _____ *has sent me to you.'" Moreover God said to Moses, "Thus you shall say to the children of* _____*: 'The* LORD *God of your fathers, the God of* _____*, the God of* _____*, and the God of* _____*, has sent me to you. This is* _____ *name forever, and this is My* _____ *to all* _____*.'"* (Exod. 3:13–15 NKJV)

From whom did God say He would deliver the children of Israel (vv. 16–17)?

MOSES AND SANDAL COVENANT

When Moses approached the burning bush, God instructed him to take off his sandals, "for the place where you stand is holy ground" (Exod. 3:5 NKJV). But that might be only part of the story.

The third of the four ancient Hebrew covenants was the inheritance covenant, also known as the sandal covenant because worn-out sandals, weighted down by rocks, were often used to mark the boundaries of the Israelites' land—and thus to mark out the next generation's inheritance. God had already entered into service (blood) and friendship (salt) covenant with Abraham, of whom (through Isaac and Jacob) He had promised to create a great nation. By commissioning Moses to take the next step and lead His people out of Egypt, perhaps God was forming sandal covenant with Moses, thus promising Moses an inheritance in God's kingdom.

Sandals, of course, also played a large part in the marriage covenant itself—the ultimate covenant of the four. Drinking wine at the wedding symbolized service to each other; sharing salted bread symbolized friendship; but a typical Hebrew groom also washed his wife's feet and put new sandals on them, thus symbolizing their joint ownership of all their property.

Remember how Christ insisted on taking off His disciples' sandals and washing their feet during the Passover Feast the night before His crucifixion, else they could not share in His inheritance? And how He said He would not drink the cup of wine until they were all together again, for what most commentators agree will be the wedding of Christ and His Bride? These gestures are part of the interlocking grid of covenant metaphors running throughout the entire Bible.

How did the Lord describe the land to which He would deliver His people (v. 17)?

What did the Lord command Moses (and through him, the elders of Israel) to do (v. 18)?

Now read verses 19–22 and fill in the blanks below:

> *"But I am sure that the king of Egypt will not let you go, no, not even by a mighty hand. So I will _____ out My hand and _____ Egypt with all My wonders which I will do in its _____; and after that he will let you go. And I will give this people _____ in the sight of the _____; and it shall be, when you go, that you shall not go _____-_____. But every woman shall ask of her _____, namely, of her who dwells near her house, articles of _____, articles of _____, and _____; and you shall put them on your sons and on your _____. So you shall _____ the Egyptians." (NKJV)*

Clearly, God already knew the heart of the Egyptian king, for everything He said about Pharaoh was about to come true. Meanwhile, what did God promise Moses that He would do once the king refused Moses' request?

In the last verse of the passage above, what did God instruct Moses to have the women of Israel ask for before they left Egypt? How do you think a major portion of this so-called plunder would eventually be used?

EXODUS 4

In verse 1, why was Moses concerned?

What were the two signs by which the Lord assured Moses that the people would believe he represented God (vv. 2–9)?

If the children of Israel still didn't believe Moses, what did God tell Moses to do next (v. 9)?

How did Moses describe himself (v. 10)? Do you think this is a fair and accurate picture of Moses, or was he making excuses?

What was the Lord's response to Moses' complaint (vv. 11–12)?

Did Moses go right away, as he was commanded (v. 13)?

Whom did the Lord agree to make the spokesman for Moses (vv. 14–16)?

What do you think of Aaron's appointment? Even though God appeared to be sending Moses all by himself, does it seem likely that He might have intended for Aaron to be part of the eventual partnership all along? Why or why not?

MOSES GOES BACK TO EGYPT

Who did Moses go to see before leaving the land of Midian to return to Egypt (v. 18)?

Why do you think he did this? Did he really need Jethro's permission? Why or why not?

Whom did Moses take with him back to Egypt?

What did the Lord command Moses to do before Pharaoh (v. 21)?

How did the Lord refer to Israel (v. 22)?

What did the Lord promise to do if Pharaoh continued to refuse to let the children of Israel go (v. 23)?

Who circumcised Moses' son (v. 25)?

What name did Zipporah call Moses (v. 26)?

This whole episode involving the "emergency" circumcision of Moses' son (it is unclear whether that son was Gershom or Eliezer), seems a little bizarre. Perhaps the most important message, to Moses, was that the time for Moses to disobey God—or even to be the least bit cavalier in his patterns of obedience—was absolutely over. He had neglected to circumcise his son at the appropriate time, several years earlier; suddenly God simply would not tolerate such carelessness anymore!

The meaning of Zipporah's expression in Exodus 4:25 ("Surely you are a husband of blood to me!" NKJV) is unclear; other translations used "bridegroom of blood," but this is no more definitive. Zipporah might have used "of blood" as a term of contempt, since she had been forced to do what Moses himself should have taken responsibility for sometime previously. On the other hand, perhaps she saw the rite of circumcision as a somewhat redeeming event by which Moses was restored to a clean relationship both with the Lord and with her.

Either way, it is likely that Zipporah and the children returned to Jethro at this time, leaving Moses to go on by himself—and thus to concentrate totally on what lay ahead. This chapter ends with Moses and Aaron meeting in the wilderness, being brought up to speed by God so that they would be wholly in accord, then meeting for the first time with the elders of the children of Israel.

Read verses 27–31 and explain in your own words how the children of Israel reacted to the message Moses and Aaron delivered from the Lord.

Knowing what you know about the children of Israel, do you think this is how they will continue to react to Moses' leadership in the days ahead?

PULLING IT ALL TOGETHER . . .

• Despite Pharaoh's decree that all male children of the Israelites should be thrown into the Nile River, Moses miraculously survived. Indeed, God worked things out so that his own mother became his officially sanctioned nursemaid, and he was adopted by the daughter of Pharaoh herself— and was then raised within the royal household of Egypt.

• As Moses grew up and became a young man, he obviously was aware that he wasn't an Egyptian by birth. One day he saw an Egyptian slave master beating one of his own people. Passion overwhelmed him, and he killed the Egyptian, only to be seen by others who threw the murder back in his face a day or two later. So Moses fled to the land of Midian to escape the wrath of Pharaoh.

• In Midian, Moses met Jethro, the local priest; married his daughter Zipporah; and settled down to the quiet life of a shepherd.

• Forty years later, God called Moses through the burning bush and commissioned him to go back to Egypt and lead God's people out of bondage.

• Moses protested that he was not a natural leader, that he had trouble speaking, and that God should call someone else. But God knew whom He wanted; His only concession was to allow Moses to team up with his brother, Aaron, so that Aaron could do the talking for both of them.

• Thus Moses returned to Egypt and told the elders of the children of Israel what God had called him to accomplish. And then the stage was set . . .

CONFRONTATION
AND STRUGGLE

3

EXODUS 5:1–12:36

Before We Begin . . .

When you think of the famous plagues of Egypt, brought on Pharaoh and his people by God Himself, which one do you think of as the most horrific?

How do you feel about God's hardening of Pharaoh's heart so that he would repeatedly refuse to let God's people go? Was this fair? Did God perhaps have a higher reason than what appears on the surface?

EXODUS 5

LET MY PEOPLE GO!

As the title of this study guide chapter suggests, the next eight chapters of Exodus break down into two major, intertwined sections. These include the monumental *confrontation* between Moses and Pharaoh with which the Exodus begins and the resulting *struggle* between Pharaoh and his magicians on one side and Moses and God on the other. The Egyptian and the Israelite peoples were also important players in everything that happened, but the real contest raged between God and the supposed might of the Egyptian nation, symbolized by Pharaoh and the servants, officials, and magicians of his court.

In the end, of course, it was really no contest at all—but the Egyptians refused to recognize what God had made inevitable, and therefore they paid a far higher price than God might have required if they had simply given Moses what he asked. On the other hand, the Egyptians had cruelly oppressed the children of God for generations, and thus much of what God brought upon them can also be seen as divine punishment for their mistreatment of His own beloved people.

Let's begin with the text of the first nine verses. Fill in the blanks below to get a sense of how the confrontation between Moses and Pharaoh began.

> *Afterward Moses and Aaron went in and told Pharaoh, "Thus says the LORD God of Israel: '_____ _____ _____ _____, that they may hold a _____ to Me in the wilderness.' " And Pharaoh said, "Who is the LORD, that I should obey His voice to let Israel go? I do not know the _____, nor will I let Israel go." So they said, "The God of the _____ has met with us. Please, let us go three days' journey into the desert and _____ to the LORD our God, lest He fall upon us with _____ or with the sword." Then the king of Egypt said to them, "Moses and Aaron, why do you take the people from their work? Get back to your _____." And Pharaoh said, "Look, the people of the land are many now, and you make them rest from their labor!" So the same day Pharaoh commanded the _____ of the people and their officers, saying, "You shall no longer give the people _____ to make brick as before. Let them go and gather straw for themselves. And you shall lay on them the quota of bricks which they made before. You shall not reduce it. For they are idle; therefore they cry out, saying, 'Let us go and sacrifice to our God.' Let more work be laid on the men, that they may labor in it, and let them not regard _____ words." (Exod. 5:1–9 NKJV)*

In the previous verses, what did Pharaoh say about the Lord? What do you think of his question—was it arrogant or just plain stupid?

For how much time did Moses and Aaron ask so that the people could travel into the desert and make sacrifices to the Lord?

What did they say might happen if they did not make those sacrifices?

Nonetheless, about what was the king of Egypt most concerned (vv. 4–5)? Whose welfare did he have in mind?

Why did Pharaoh instruct his taskmasters and officers to stop providing the children of Israel with straw to make bricks and instead insist that the people gather the straw themselves?

What did Pharaoh call the people in verse 8—and then again in verse 17?

Clearly, Pharaoh's initial response to the word of the Lord, spoken through Moses, wasn't favorable. It also wasn't very wise—but of course, Pharaoh didn't know this yet. He still believed his own gods and magicians were as powerful as the God of the Israelites, who created all things.

Verses 22–23 give us a typical interchange between Moses and God. We mentioned these in the introduction to this study guide. Here, Moses acts true to form and *asks* the Lord why He's doing what He's doing, rather than blaming God or absolving himself.

> So Moses returned to the LORD and said, "Lord, why have You brought trouble on this people? Why is it You have sent me? For since I came to Pharaoh to speak in Your name, he has done evil to this people; neither have You delivered Your people at all." (Exod. 5:22–23 NKJV)

What did Moses say the Lord had allowed to happen to His people?

EXODUS 6

GOD RENEWS HIS PROMISE TO ISRAEL

Chapter 6 begins with the Lord's response to Moses' questions. Fill in the blanks below to see what He said.

> Then the LORD said to Moses, "Now you shall see what I will do to _____. For with a _____ _____ he will let them _____, and with a _____ _____ he will _____ them out of his _____." (Exod. 6:1 NKJV)

Next, God explains something to Moses about His own name, which we will examine elsewhere in this chapter in the sidebar entitled "The Names of God." As we will see in chapter 6 of this study guide, in Exodus 34:5–8 God also reveals His thirteen attributes to Moses. Meanwhile, read the remainder of Exodus 6 and answer the questions below.

What did God "hear" and "keep" (v. 5)?

Who kept the children of Israel in bondage?

What four things did the Lord promise to do for the children of Israel (v. 6)?

1.

2.

3.

4.

How did the Lord say that the children of Israel would know that He was their God (v. 7)?

What did the Lord promise to give to the children of Israel as an eternal heritage (v. 8)?

THE NAMES OF GOD

In Exodus 6:2–8, God spoke the following words to Moses: *And God spoke to Moses and said to him: "I am the LORD. I appeared to Abraham, to Isaac, and to Jacob, as God Almighty, but by My name LORD I was not known to them. I have also established My covenant with them, to give them the land of Canaan, the land of their pilgrimage, in which they were strangers. And I have also heard the groaning of the children of Israel whom the Egyptians keep in bondage, and I have remembered My covenant. Therefore say to the children of Israel: 'I am the LORD; I will bring you out from under the burdens of the Egyptians, I will rescue you from their bondage, and I will redeem you with an outstretched arm and with great judgments. I will take you as My people, and I will be your God. Then you shall know that I am the LORD your God who brings you out from under the burdens of the Egyptians. And I will bring you into the land which I swore to give to Abraham, Isaac, and Jacob; and I will give it to you as a heritage: I am the LORD.' "*

Entire books have been written about the different names of God, which appear at various places in the Scriptures, so we won't attempt to go into detail on this subject here. But what does God mean, specifically, in the above quotation? Was He not also known to Abraham, Isaac, and Jacob as YHWH (often written as "Yahweh"), which essentially means "Lord"?

The answer is yes—He was. But primarily, God appeared to these earlier patriarchs as their Sustainer and Provider. It seems that God wanted to make it very clear to Moses that He was now showing the children of Israel another side of Himself, that of the Promise Keeper who would not only sustain and provide for them, but also bring to fruition all the promises He had ever made to them and their ancestors.

And this, of course, is exactly what He did.

Why didn't the children of Israel heed Moses' words (v. 9)?

What did the Lord then instruct Moses to tell Pharaoh (vv. 10–11)? Even so, why did Moses believe that Pharaoh would not listen to him?

THE FAMILY OF MOSES AND AARON

Verses 14–26 can seem somewhat puzzling, for at first glance they seem so out of place in the middle of the bondage/deliverance narrative. Suddenly God halts all the action and gives us a lesson in genealogy!

But the Lord never does anything without a reason, and this insert is no exception. Undoubtedly He wanted to make absolutely sure that future generations would know exactly who Moses and Aaron were, both in terms of their reputation as obedient servants who served Him faithfully for many years and in terms of their earthly ancestry. Thus He makes it clear that the two brothers are direct descendants of Abraham, Isaac, and Jacob through the lineage of Levi, Jacob's third son. To the tribe of Levi, God eventually gave the priesthood, beginning with Aaron and extending down through the generations, even to those who still trace their ancestry back to the Levites today.

We have chosen not to ask questions based on this passage, because remembering the names of many of these people is simply not as important as understanding what happened. Perhaps it is enough to note how God Himself explained what He was doing in the last two verses of this section:

> *These are the same Aaron and Moses to whom the LORD said, "Bring out the children of Israel from the land of Egypt according to their armies." These are the ones who spoke to Pharaoh king of Egypt, to bring out the children of Israel from Egypt. These are the same Moses and Aaron. (Exod. 6:26–27 NKJV)*

The last two verses of this chapter set us up for what happens next.

What did the Lord say to Moses (v. 29)?

What did Moses say he had (v. 30)?

EXODUS 7

MOSES BEFORE PHARAOH

In this chapter we begin to encounter the famous ten plagues, used by God both to punish the Egyptians and to convince Pharaoh to let the children of Israel go. Unfortunately for Pharaoh, it took a lot of convincing. On the other hand, we know that the Lord purposely hardened Pharaoh's heart to demonstrate His omnipotence and to bring about His justice.

Read through chapter 7 and answer the following questions.

What did the Lord call Moses and Aaron (v. 1)? By using these designations—or "titles"—do you think the Lord was taking a chance on instilling too much pride in His two servants?

What did the Lord instruct Moses' brother to tell Pharaoh (v. 2)?

The Lord said He would harden Pharaoh's heart . . . and then do what (v. 3)?

Who would know that God is Lord (v. 5)?

How old were Moses and Aaron when they spoke to Pharaoh (v. 7)?

AARON'S MIRACULOUS ROD

What instructions did the Lord give Moses and Aaron (v. 9)?

What happened to Aaron's rod when he obeyed the Lord and did as he was commanded (v. 10)?

Were Pharaoh's sorcerers able to imitate the Lord's miracle?

What happened to their serpents (v. 12)?

Given all the above, did Pharaoh's heart then grow soft toward the children of Israel?

THE FIRST PLAGUE: WATERS TURNED TO BLOOD

Where did the Lord instruct Moses to go (v. 15)?

What did the Lord say would happen to the river?

In addition to the Nile River, what other bodies of water in Egypt were affected (v. 19)?

When Moses and Aaron did as they were commanded, what happened?

How was Pharaoh's heart affected?

How did the Egyptians find water to drink (v. 24)?

How long did the water remain blood?

EXODUS 8

THE SECOND PLAGUE: FROGS

Now begins the pattern that would hold true through the next eight plagues. In each case, Pharaoh either refuses to let the children of Israel go in spite of the punishment God brings, or he puts impossible conditions on their exit. Or, as in this case, he agrees to let them go but changes his mind as soon as the plague-of-the-moment stops.

Read Exodus 8 and answer the following questions.

What did the Lord say would happen to Pharaoh's territory if he did not let the children of Israel go?

Where did God say the frogs would go when they arrived (vv. 3–4)?

When Aaron did as he was commanded, what happened (v. 6)?

Were the magicians successful in copying the Lord's miracle (v. 7)?

What day did Moses say the frogs would be gone from the land (v. 10)?

Would the frogs go completely away, never to be seen again (v. 11)? If not, where would they go?

Did the Lord keep Moses' word to Pharaoh (v. 13)?

As soon as the frogs were removed, what did Pharaoh do (vv. 14–15)?

THE THIRD PLAGUE: LICE

As before, when Aaron did what he was commanded, what happened (v. 17)?

Were the magicians successful this time in copying the Lord's miracle? What does this suggest to you about the nature of the plagues God was now bringing?

What was Pharaoh's response (v. 19)?

THE FOURTH PLAGUE: FLIES

What did the Lord do (v. 24)?

Where did Pharaoh suggest that the children of Israel should make sacrifices to the Lord (v. 25)?

Why did Moses turn down Pharaoh's offer (v. 26)?

How many days' journey into the wilderness did Moses say the people would travel (v. 27)?

What agreement did Moses make with Pharaoh (v. 29)?

Was Pharaoh's heart finally softened after the Lord removed the swarms of flies (vv. 30–32)?

Exodus 9

The Fifth Plague: Diseased Livestock

According to verses 2–3, if Pharaoh still refused to let the Lord's people go, what would be affected this time?

Fill in the blanks below to see what God did for His people.

"And the _____ will make a difference between the _____ of _____ and the _____ of _____. So nothing shall _____ of all that _____ to the _____ of Israel." Then the _____ appointed a set _____, saying, "_____ the LORD will do this _____ in the _____." (Exod. 9:4–5 NKJV)

What happened the next day—and what effect did it have on Pharaoh?

The Sixth Plague: Boils

What did the Lord instruct Moses and Aaron to do (v. 8)?

What did the dust turn into (vv. 9–10)?

Why do you believe the Lord would ask Moses and Aaron to play such central roles in each of the plagues?

Why couldn't Pharaoh's magicians repeat this miracle (v. 11)?

Did this plague finally soften Pharaoh's heart?

THE SEVENTH PLAGUE: HAIL

According to verses 13–19, if Pharaoh did not let the Lord's people go, what did the Lord say He would do to cause the people of Egypt and their livestock to die?

What did the Lord instruct Moses to do (v. 22)?

In addition to the hail, what also "darted to the ground" and mingled with the hail after Moses stretched out his rod toward heaven (vv. 23–24)?

Where in Egypt did the children of Israel live (v. 26)?

Fill in the blanks below to see if Pharaoh repented.

> *And _____ sent and called for _____ and*
> *Aaron, and said to them, "I have _____ this time.*
> *The LORD is _____, and my people and I are*
> *_____." (Exod. 9:27 NKJV)*

Did Pharaoh agree to let the children of Israel go (v. 28)?

What agreement did Moses make with Pharaoh (v. 29)?

Why were the wheat and spelt "spared"?

When Moses left the city, what did he do (v. 33)?

Had Pharaoh's heart truly softened yet (vv. 34–35)?

EXODUS 10

THE EIGHTH PLAGUE: LOCUSTS

Now we come to plagues eight and nine. Number eight is not entirely unfamiliar, even in modern days. Yet it's unlikely that any locust plague, in any time or place, has been worse than what Pharaoh brought upon Egypt by his refusal to humble himself before the one true God and do as He commanded.

Read chapter 10 and work through the following questions.

What question did Aaron and Moses ask Pharaoh (v. 3)?

What did they say would happen to the Egyptian people if he did not let the children of Israel go?

What did Pharaoh's servants say to him (v. 7)?

Did Pharaoh agree to let the children of Israel go (vv. 10–11)?

When Moses did what he was commanded, what happened (vv. 12–13)?

What did the locusts do (v. 15)?

Fill in the blanks below to see if Pharaoh repented.

> *Then _____ called for Moses and Aaron in _____, and said, "I have _____ against the _____ your _____ and against _____. Now therefore, please _____ my _____ only this once, and _____ the* LORD *your _____, that He may take away from _____ this _____ only." (Exod. 10:16–17 NKJV)*

When it was finally over, to where did the Lord blow the locusts away?

Was Pharaoh finally willing to let the children of Israel go (v. 20)?

THE NINTH PLAGUE: DARKNESS

When Moses did what he was commanded, what happened (v. 22)?

How many days did the land of Egypt lay in total darkness?

What did Moses instruct Pharaoh to do (v. 25)?
Did Moses agree to leave his flock with Pharaoh?

Was Pharaoh's heart softened by the Lord (v. 27)?

How accurate was Moses' prediction in verse 29? In other words, did he ever see Pharaoh's face again?

EXODUS 11

DEATH OF THE FIRSTBORN ANNOUNCED

The segue from the end of chapter 10 to the beginning of chapter 11 is a little problematic, demonstrating that many chapter divisions in God's Word, introduced after the originals were written, are entirely arbitrary. The most logical way to read this particular section is to assume that what Moses had to say in Exodus 11:4–8 was part of his last confrontation with Pharaoh—after which he "went out from Pharaoh in great anger" (v. 8 NKJV).

We are told that Moses was highly esteemed by both the Egyptian people and by the officials who were part of Pharaoh's court, certainly to some extent because of the plagues Moses had warned them about—which then came true with such devastating results.

In verse 1, the Lord promised Moses that this would be the last plague. After this, He said that Pharaoh would do what?

What did God instruct the Israelites to collect (v. 2)? Why would He want them to do this?

What would happen at midnight in the land of Egypt (vv. 4–5)?

Why did the Lord continue to harden Pharaoh's heart (vv. 9–10)?

EXODUS 12

GOD ESTABLISHES THE PASSOVER

For a longer discussion of the Passover itself, please see the sidebar in this chapter entitled "The Meaning of Passover." Meanwhile, please read chapter 12 and answer the following questions.

What did the Lord command every man to do on the tenth of the month (v. 3)?

Describe the lamb and explain how it was to be killed. Who was to kill it?

What was to happen to the blood? How was the meat to be pre-pared?

Whom did God say would pass through the land of Egypt and strike the firstborn of all those without blood on their doorposts (v. 12)?

What was the Lord's commandment with respect to the Passover Feast (v. 14)?

Read Exodus 12:15–20. In your own words, summarize the Lord's commandments to the children of Israel with regard to the Feast of Unleavened Bread. (Note: It is possible to break these down in different ways, but look for at least four distinct com-mandments.)

1.

2.

3.

4.

What did Moses instruct the elders of Israel to do (vv. 21–22)?

THE MEANING OF PASSOVER

Probably no holy day is better known and more beloved than Passover. On a one-person-versus-God basis, Yom Kippur might be a more solemn and more personally meaningful holy day, but Yom Kippur, Rosh Hashanah, Shavuot, and even Firstfruits all remain relatively unknown among non-Jews. In contrast, more and more non-Jewish congregations every year are beginning to organize and celebrate Passover seders (pronounced *say'-der*, not *cedar*!), often with Jewish friends helping to organize, lead, and explain each of the many longstanding Passover traditions.

Passover is the day on which the Jews remember their deliverance from Egypt. It marks the beginning of the Jewish new year and always occurs on the fourteenth day of Nisan (the first month of the Hebrew calendar), corresponding to March or April.

The Hebrew word for Passover is *Pesach (Pay'-sock)*, meaning "to pass or jump over." The final letter in the Hebrew alphabet, *tav*, is shaped like a cross and literally means "a sign of the covenant." The same shape was (and often still is) embodied within the two sticks arranged in the shape of a cross inside the body cavity of a Pesach lamb to hold it open during roasting.

Jesus, of course, was crucified on Passover. Tradition has it that He died at exactly the same hour that the last of each year's Passover lambs were slain by the high priest. The same priest said, *"Nagmar!"* (meaning "It is finished!") at the moment of the last lamb's death; these were Christ's final words as well, as recorded in John 19:30.

Jesus rose, of course, on the Feast of Firstfruits, which occurs on the day following the first Sabbath after Passover, during an eight-day period that begins with Passover and is known as the Week of Unleavened Bread. These three holidays, collectively, form what the ancient Hebrews called an *echad*, or a unity. The obvious comparison can be made to God—Father, Son, and Holy Spirit. Or to an individual—body, soul, and spirit. Or to soul all by itself—intellect, emotions, and will.

In ancient Hebrew, Egypt was known as *Mitzraim*, literally "a straight and narrow place; a birth canal." Many scholars believe that Christ was referring to this concept when He spoke of being born again in the Spirit:

Enter by the narrow gate; for wide is the gate and broad is the way that leads to destruction, and there are many who go in by it. Because narrow is the gate and difficult is the way which leads to life, and there are few who find it. (Matt. 7:13-14 NKJV)

In Hebrew understanding, on the shore of the Red Sea the waters broke and the people of Israel passed through a birth canal. Many historians thus maintain that the children of Israel were born as a nation, and as a free people, at the exact moment when they were "delivered" on the far shore of the Red Sea.

In Moses' time, the Passover was not just for those descended from Abraham, Isaac, and Jacob. Instead, it was given for the whole assembly of the congregation of Israel, which included Egyptians and people from other nations living in Egypt who chose to join themselves to God's people. Modern Christians tend to think that the twelve tribes of Israel left Egypt by themselves, but many Gentile people also left with the Israelites, forming a mixed multitude (Exodus 12:38).

Read Exodus 12:23–28. In your own words, describe the Passover sacrifice and explain why it is necessary to remember it throughout all generations.

THE TENTH PLAGUE: DEATH OF THE FIRSTBORN

Just as the Lord promised, what happened at midnight (12:29–30)?

THE EXODUS

Why did Pharaoh call for Moses and Aaron—and what did he urge them to do (12:31–33)?

What did the Egyptians give the children of Israel before they left (vv. 35–36)?

PULLING IT ALL TOGETHER . . .

• God sent Moses and Aaron, together, to demand that Pharaoh let God's people go.

• They warned Pharaoh repeatedly that Egypt would suffer horrific consequences if he refused their demands.

• Nonetheless, even though he came close to relenting several times, Pharaoh stiffened his resolve (and God hardened his heart) nine separate times before he finally gave in.

• It took ten plagues, including waters turned to blood, frogs, lice, flies, diseased livestock, boils, hail, locusts, darkness, and finally the death of the firstborn of each Egyptian family—including Pharaoh's own son—to convince Pharaoh to do the right thing. In the process, God severely punished Egypt for their vile mistreatment of God's people.

DELIVERANCE

EXODUS 12:37–18:27

Before We Begin . . .

Of all the well-known events that occurred during the Exodus itself, which one do you remember the best? Is it the crossing of the Red Sea? The manna from heaven?

What are your thoughts about Moses' leadership ability, heading into the Exodus? How do you think he will do as his responsibilities increase?

EXODUS 12:37–51

The last fifteen verses of Exodus 12 tell us what happened when Pharaoh finally relented. He even demanded that the children of Israel leave, as did many others among the Egyptians—gladly giving them valuable jewelry and clothing if they would *just go!* This fulfilled God's promise to Abraham, made hundreds of years earlier, wherein God said:

> *"Know certainly that your descendants will be strangers in a land that is not theirs, and will serve them, and they will afflict them four hundred years. And also the nation whom they serve I will judge; afterward they shall come out with great possessions." (Gen. 15:13–14 NKJV)*

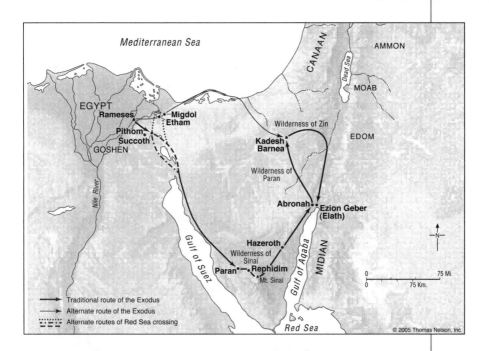

Pharaoh was even so humbled by the true God that he asked Moses and Aaron to bless *him*, back in Exodus 8:28 during the plague of the flies—although that brief flash of humility did not last.

We are told later on (Exodus 38:26; Numbers 1:46; 2:32) that the number of Israelite men was 603,550. But this number does not include women and children, which undoubtedly brought the total number of Israelites to more than two million people. And this number, of course, did not include the non-Israelites who went with them, of whom it is impossible to get an exact count.

The movie *The Ten Commandments* makes a grand spectacle of the Exodus itself, with everyone dressed in colorful costumes, moving out briskly in joyful celebration, in bright sunlight. In truth, perhaps, only the speed and the joy reflect reality, for it's unlikely that either their costumes or their attitudes were quite as colorful as we might like to imagine.

And almost certainly the sun was not high, for above all else they were in a hurry to get moving. When the dam of Pharaoh's resistance finally broke, they got under way so quickly they didn't even have time to bake their bread but took unleavened dough instead and baked it en route. On that first day, they journeyed from Rameses, the city in which they were apparently concentrated and ready to go, to a place called Succoth, near present-day Lake Timsah.

Moses summed up all this, with special emphasis in verse 42 on the night of solemn observance to the Lord, in this passage:

> Now the sojourn of the children of Israel who lived in Egypt was four hundred and thirty years. And it came to pass at the end of the four hundred and thirty years—on that very same day—it came to pass that all the armies of the LORD went out from the land of Egypt. It is a night of solemn observance to the LORD for bringing them out of the land of Egypt. This is that night of the LORD, a solemn observance for all the children of Israel throughout their generations. (Exod. 12:40–42 NKJV)

The comparison calendar on the next page shows the relationship between the Jewish calendar, which remains unchanged since biblical times, and the Gregorian calendar adopted by most of the rest of the world in AD 1582 after a decree issued by Pope Gregory. The "Special Days" column includes the seven sacred festivals ordained by God, beginning with Passover (all of which are further explained in Leviticus 23). It also includes two traditional Jewish holidays, the Feast of Dedication (commonly called Hanukkah) observed by Christ Himself in John 10:22, and Purim, the annual celebration of Esther's role in preserving the Jews. Many scholars believe that Christ's attendance at the Feast of Dedication reinforces His teaching (and Paul's, too) to the effect that man-made traditions are fine as long as they do not conflict with God's decrees.

Gregorian Calendar	Jewish Calendar	Agricultural Connection	Special Days
March–April	Month 1: Nisan	Latter rains Barley harvest Flax harvest	(1) Nisan 14: Passover Exod. 12:1–11; Lev. 23:5 (2) Nisan 15–21: Unleavened Bread Lev. 23:6–8 (3) Nisan 21: Firstfruits Lev. 23:9–14
April–May	Month 2: Iyyar	Beginning of dry season	
May–June	Month 3: Sivan	Ripening of early figs Vine tending	(4) Sivan 6 (50 days after Firstfruits): Shavuot (called Pentecost in New Testament) Lev. 23:15–22
June–July	Month 4: Tammuz	Wheat harvest Ripening of first grapes	
July–August	Month 5: Ab	Grape harvest	
August–September	Month 6: Elul	Dates and summer figs	
September–October	Month 7: Tishri	Early rains	(5) Tishri 1: Feast of Trumpets Lev. 23:23–25 (6) Tishri 10: Day of Atonement Lev. 16; 23:26–32 (7) Tishri 15–21: Feast of Tabernacles Lev. 23:33–36
October–November	Month 8: Marchesvan	Plowing Olive harvest	(8) Kislev 25: Feast of Dedication (Hanukkah) John 10:22 (Not ordained by God)
November–December	Month 9: Kislev	Grape planting	
December–January	Month 10: Tebeth	Latter rains	
January–February	Month 11: Shebat	Blossoming of almond trees	
February–March	Month 12: Adar	Citrus fruit harvest	(9) Adar 13–14: Purim Esther 9:26–28 (Not ordained by God)

Passover Regulations

In the final verses of chapter 12, Moses recapped the Lord's words to Aaron, detailing again God's regulations for the Passover. Read these eight verses carefully, and see how many separate regulations you can list below—perhaps up to seven!

1.

2.

3.

4.

5.

6.

7.

Exodus 13

Almost literally, as soon as God brought the children of Israel out of Egypt, He began establishing with them the relationship that He desired. Think back to the original blood covenant that God made with Abraham in Genesis 15:1–17. God required very little in return for His promise to make of Abraham's descendants a great nation, and neither did He place huge expectations on the shoulders of Isaac and Jacob.

But now things begin to change as the Lord begins to mold and develop His people.

What did the Lord command of Moses (vv. 1–2)? Why do you think He did so? BECAUSE THEY WERE THE CARED SEED to REPRODUCE the faith

Why did Moses tell the children of Israel that they should remember that particular day? the day that they LEFT SLAVERY AND the Lord LEAd them out

What was the name of the month? A bib

What did the Lord call the Promised Land (v. 5)? A LANd flowing with MiLK & HONEY

How many days did Moses tell the people they should eat unleavened bread before the actual feast (v. 6)? 7

What were the instructions—and the reason—given by the Lord for the use of unleavened bread (vv. 8–10)? it was what the Lord did for ME when I came out of Eygpt, I was A sign to keep for year after year

THE LAW OF THE FIRSTBORN

Read verses 11–16. Explain in your own words why you believe the Lord insisted on having the firstborn of every creature redeemed to Him. To see if they will KEEP the faith. That he lead them out to keep them faithful.

Why did the Lord lead His people through the wilderness instead of going through the land of the Philistines, which would have been a shorter route (vv. 17–18)? So they had a long way if they were to give up and return to slavery

Whose bones did Moses take with him? Joesph

The Lord stayed with the children of Israel for their entire journey. In what visual form did He travel with them by day, and in what visual form by night (vv. 21–22)? pillar of a cloud & pillar of fire

EXODUS 14

THE RED SEA CROSSING

Chapter 14 details what might be the best-known miracle in the Bible—certainly one that is right up there with the water being turned into wine and the various healings Jesus brought about in the New Testament. For a bit more insight into the Red Sea miracle, see "Was It Really the Red Sea?" on the next page. Meanwhile, read Exodus 14 and answer the following questions.

Why did the Lord instruct the children of Israel to camp between Migdol and the sea (vv. 1–4)? The For the Pharaoh will say they are wandering aimlessly the wilderness has closed them of s

Did Pharaoh behave as the Lord said he would (vv. 5–9)?

YES

Why were the children of Israel afraid?

YES

WAS IT REALLY THE RED SEA?

Much has been made, in recent times, about whether the children of Israel actually crossed through what we know today as the Red Sea. Many scholars argue that they could not possibly have traveled far enough south to reach the modern Red Sea in one day.

Two or three facts, however, are certain. First, the original Hebrew refers to the *Yam Suph*. *Yam* is the ordinary Hebrew word for "sea," and *suph* is the word for "reeds" or "rushes." This is the same word used earlier in Exodus 2:3, 5, to refer to what Moses' basket was placed "among" when it was put into the Nile River.

Second, the translation of this phrase as "Red Sea" was introduced into the English Bible via the King James Version, which in turn was based on the second-century BC Greek Septuagint and the Latin Vulgate, which came somewhat later. "Red Sea" then became the traditional translation of the Hebrew words (just as the name "Jacob," Jesus' brother, became "James") and has come down to us in the twenty-first century as "fact."

So, what body of water *did* the children of Israel pass through? The first simple truth is that no one knows for sure. And the second simple truth is that it really doesn't matter. God separated the waters and created dry land for His people to cross over to safety; those waters were deep enough to drown the Egyptian army when the waters returned after the Egyptians tried to follow.

Which waters they were is probably something we'll have to ask God Himself when we see Him in person!

To conclude this chapter, read verses 15–31. Describe in your own words this well-known scene in biblical history. What happened? The ~~Pah~~ Pharaoh did as the Lord knew he would. And was distorted

EXODUS 15

Chapter 15 contains two songs of jubilation—the Song of Moses and the Song of Miriam, his sister. Rather than asking questions about the text itself, let us look at the first of these two in "structural" terms to see how it fits together.

In the reproduction below we have purposely broken Moses' song into its three main sections, comprising verses 1–6, 7–11, and 12–16, followed by the conclusion in verses 17–18. Notice how each of the main sections ends with a clear statement of praise to the Lord, two of which refer to His powerful right hand and/or His arm—which, of course, are metaphors for the vast reserves of honor and strength with which He protects His own.

THE SONG OF MOSES

Section 1

¹*Then Moses and the children of Israel sang this song to the LORD, and spoke, saying:*

"I will sing to the LORD,

For He has triumphed gloriously!

The horse and its rider

He has thrown into the sea!

²*The LORD is my strength and song,*

And He has become my salvation;

He is my God, and I will praise Him;

My father's God, and I will exalt Him.

³*The LORD is a man of war;*

The L ORD *is His name.*

4Pharaoh's chariots and his army He has cast into the sea;

His chosen captains also are drowned in the Red Sea.

5The depths have covered them;

They sank to the bottom like a stone.

6Your right hand, O L ORD, has become glorious in power;

Your right hand, O L ORD, has dashed the enemy in pieces."

Section 2

7"And in the greatness of Your excellence

You have overthrown those who rose against You;

You sent forth Your wrath;

It consumed them like stubble.

8And with the blast of Your nostrils

The waters were gathered together;

The floods stood upright like a heap;

The depths congealed in the heart of the sea.

9The enemy said, 'I will pursue,

I will overtake,

I will divide the spoil;

My desire shall be satisfied on them.

I will draw my sword,

My hand shall destroy them.'

10You blew with Your wind,

The sea covered them;

They sank like lead in the mighty waters.

11Who is like You, O L ORD, among the gods?

Who is like You, glorious in holiness,

Fearful in praises, doing wonders?"

Section 3

¹²*"You stretched out Your right hand;*

The earth swallowed them.

¹³*You in Your mercy have led forth*

The people whom You have redeemed;

You have guided them in Your strength

To Your holy habitation.

¹⁴*The people will hear and be afraid;*

Sorrow will take hold of the inhabitants of Philistia.

¹⁵*Then the chiefs of Edom will be dismayed;*

The mighty men of Moab,

Trembling will take hold of them;

All the inhabitants of Canaan will melt away.

¹⁶*Fear and dread will fall on them;*

By the greatness of Your arm

They will be as still as a stone,

Till Your people pass over, O Lord,

Till the people pass over

Whom You have purchased."

Conclusion

¹⁷*"You will bring them in and plant them*

In the mountain of Your inheritance,

In the place, O Lord, which You have made

For Your own dwelling,

The sanctuary, O Lord, which Your hands have established.

¹⁸*The Lord shall reign forever and ever."*

Verses 19–21 repeat the reasons for Moses' song, then include Miriam's response, known as the Song of Miriam. Miriam and all the other women sang and danced (see "Too Old to Dance?" below), with "timbrels," or tambourines, in a scene that must have been a tremendous joy to behold!

TOO OLD TO DANCE?

Moses was eighty years old at the time of the Exodus. Aaron was eighty-three. Therefore, since Miriam was a young girl when Moses was born, she was probably in her early nineties when she and the women with her danced and sang her jubilant response to Moses' song of triumph over the Egyptians. Imagine dancing and singing at the age of ninety-plus!

BITTER WATERS MADE SWEET

Please read the remaining six verses of chapter 15 and answer the following questions.

How many days did the children of Israel go without water (vv. 22–24)? 3 days

How did the bitter waters become sweet? 15-25
They thur A tree into the water

What statute and ordinance did God make at Marah?
HE tested them. Give ear & sight to his commandments and all of his statutes. He would not the diseases on them as he did the Egyptians

65

EXODUS 16

BREAD FROM HEAVEN

This chapter tells us how God fed the children of Israel when they were in the wilderness. Please read it and respond to the following questions.

How long had the children of Israel been in the desert when they came to the Wilderness of Sin (v. 1)?

The 15th Day of the second Month

What was their next complaint?

Of food

What kind of food did the Lord provide (v. 4)?

BREAd

Against whom did Moses explain that the children of Israel were actually complaining (vv. 6–8)?

Our Lord

Why do you think God rewarded Israel's complaining by feeding them (v. 8)? To Show them He HAS the power to do for them

How did the Lord appear to the congregation (v. 10)?

In the Cloud

What came up at evening and covered the camp for the congregation to eat (v. 13)?

Quail

What appeared on the ground in the morning for the congregation to eat (vv. 14–15)?

A fine flake like thing bread

The Lord established what law to be observed on the Sabbath (vv. 29–30)?

He gave them 2 days wroth of bread on saturday and to rest on the seventh day

What did the children of Israel call the bread they found on the ground on every morning except the Sabbath (v. 31)? What did it taste like?

Manna - it was like coriander seed white, And its taste was like wafers and honey

Previous verses indicate how easily and quickly the manna spoiled. According to verses 32–33, the Lord commanded Israel to keep an omer *of manna (about two quarts) to show generations to come, which we must assume He intended to prevent from spoiling. In your own words, explain whether you think this would be a miracle. And if it was, why do you think the Lord would bring it about?*

It was a miracle to show How He fed the people in need At the present time and so people to see As time went on.

Verse 34 tells us that "Aaron laid [the manna] up before the Testimony, to be kept." What does this mean—how was "the Testimony" kept, or preserved? *IN A JAR*

How many years did the children of Israel live in the wilderness, eating manna? *40 YEARS*

EXODUS 17

WATER FROM THE ROCK

The children of Israel again complained about not having water (vv. 1–4). This time, Moses asked them why they tempted the Lord. What did he mean by this? Surely it was not wrong to want water . . . was it? Or was something else going on? *THEY COMPLAINED OF LEAVING ESYPT AND DYING FROM NO WATER*

How did the Lord provide water (vv. 5–6)? *HAVING MOSES TO STRIKE THE ROCK WITH HIS STAFF*

VICTORY OVER THE AMALEKITES

Verses 8–13 describe a battle between Israel and the Amalekites, in which the Lord delivered victory to Israel. What well-known Israelite leader is mentioned for the first time in the Bible (v. 9)?

AMALEK

Verse 12 indicates that Moses' hands needed to be supported to hold up his rod. Why was it so important to keep the rod lifted up? To mhintain the power

What was the name of the altar Moses built (v. 15)? What does this name mean? The Lord is My Banner

Exodus 18

The Appointment of Judges

This chapter reintroduces Moses' father-in-law, Jethro, who hears of what Moses and the children of Israel have been doing and comes out into the desert to see for himself. Many scholars believe that God specifically sent Jethro at this particular time, to this particular place, in direct response to a situation that had been developing between Moses and the children of Israel for some time. Read through this chapter and answer the following questions to see what that situation was—and how Jethro's advice turned out to be so helpful to Moses.

Do verses 1–7 mean that Moses was in the desert with the children of Israel without his wife and children? Yes

Verses 13–16 tell us that Moses was essentially serving as the sole judge over all the disputes that arose, inevitably, among the millions of people he was leading. Why did Jethro object to this setup (vv. 17–18)? Too much hardship on Moses

In your own words, what did Jethro tell Moses to do (vv. 19–23)? What modern-management term (or terms) would you use to describe what Jethro suggested? DELEGATION

A GOVERNTERING Body MANAGE MENT

Did Moses follow his father-in-law's advice? And if so, did it turn out to be good advice? yES

MANAGEMENT 101

The story of Jethro and his advice to Moses provides a fascinating insight into Moses' development as a leader. Clearly, God used Jethro to teach Moses the concept of *delegation,* which all modern students of management agree is the only way to fly. It's the fundamental concept behind management by objective, management by commitment, just-in-time inventory management, and countless other extrapolations. You cannot do everything yourself; if you would command a large corps of followers, you *must* learn to delegate authority. And that's exactly what Moses finally learned to do.

PULLING IT ALL TOGETHER . . .

• About six hundred thousand men came out of Egypt with Moses—but that's only part of the story! In all, more than two million descendants of Abraham, Isaac, and Jacob escaped Egyptian bondage, plus a huge number of additional "sojourners" who came out with them. Many of these soon circumcised themselves and became "grafted" into the nation of Israel.

• Among the first regulations God gave to His children were the rules regarding how and when to observe Passover. The next group of regulations dealt with consecrating the first-born to Him and observing the Feast of Unleavened Bread.

• God delivered the children of Israel from the Egyptians, for the final time, by parting the Red Sea and allowing the Israelites to cross over unharmed. This miracle has long been one of the best known in the Bible.

• Once the Israelites were safely past the Red Sea, both Moses and his sister, Miriam, led the people in jubilant songs of praise to the Lord.

• Though they were in the desert without food and water, God sent water, manna, and quail to feed the children of Israel.

• God gave the Israelites their first military victory, over the Amalekites, via the military skills of Joshua.

• God sent Jethro into the desert to observe how Moses was handling "internal affairs" among the children of Israel. Jethro gave Moses invaluable advice and changed the way Moses conducted much of his daily business.

5 COVENANT AND LAW

EXODUS 19:1–31:18

Before We Begin . . .

What is your understanding about why God gave the Ten Commandments to the children of Israel on Mount Sinai—and not to the rest of the nations on earth? Granted, they were His chosen people, but why should that matter? Have not these same Ten Commandments become a fundamental part of Western civilization? Why, then, should they have been given to just one group of people?

How do you believe God actually "gave" the Ten Commandments—and other instructions, as well—to Moses? Did He literally speak to him? If so, what qualified Moses to be in God's presence?

EXODUS 19

ISRAEL AT MOUNT SINAI

Surely Mount Sinai is one of the most familiar locations in the Bible, for this is where some of the most important events in all of history took place. It was also known as Mount Horeb. Taken together, Sinai/Horeb is mentioned sixty-one times in the New King James Version of the Bible, and close to the same number in all other modern translations.

Moses encountered the burning bush on Mount Horeb at the very beginning of his call to leadership of the children of Israel. Later on he spoke face-to-face with the God of Israel and received the Ten Commandments on top of the same mountain, then called Mount Sinai. No wonder Horeb and Sinai, by either name, were both called "the mountain of God."

These twelve chapters from Exodus tell us of Moses' major encounters with God on Mount Sinai. They detail the giving of the Ten Commandments, but they also describe the giving of the additional instructions that God presented to Moses, by which the children of Israel were to govern almost every aspect of their daily lives from the time they entered into covenant with Him.

These instructions, in particular, included detailed directions for the construction of the portable tabernacle the Israelites would carry with them throughout their wilderness trek. They also dealt with the priestly garments to be worn by Aaron and his sons, the sacred implements of worship they would use, and the well-known Ark of the Covenant that would eventually hold the original tablets of stone containing the Ten Commandments, written by the finger of God.

Those same instructions also introduce us to an artisan named Bezalel, unknown until that moment, who would fashion of pure gold the massive lampstand, about six feet tall, that stood just outside the Holy of Holies. Many years later this became perhaps the most easily recognized symbol of the reborn nation of Israel in modern times—the golden, seven-branch menorah.

But that comes toward the end of this section. Let us take it one chapter at a time. Please read Exodus 19 and answer the following questions.

After the children of Israel left Egypt, how long did it take them to reach the Wilderness of Sinai and camp before the mountain (v. 1)?

Read verses 3–6. Then fill in the blanks to discover what God meant by "special treasure" in verse 5.

And Moses went up to Mt Sinai, *and the* LORD *called to him from the mountain, saying, "* This you shall say to the House

you shall say to the _house_ of _Jacob_, and tell the children of Israel: '_You_ have seen what I did to the _Egyptian_, and how I bore you on _Eagles_ _wings_ and brought you to _Myself_. Now therefore, if you will indeed _obey_ My _voice_ and keep My _covenant_, then you shall be a _possession_ _____ to Me above all people; for all the _earth_ is Mine. And you shall be to Me a _kingdom_ of _priests_ and a _holy_ nation.' These are the words which _You_ shall speak to the _sons_ of _Israel_." (Exod. 19:3–6 NKJV)

In your own words, what do you think God meant by a "kingdom of priests and a holy nation" (v. 6)?

His chosen

What did the children of Israel commit to do (v. 8)?

we will do

What did the Lord instruct the people to do to their clothes (v. 10)? ~~let~~ wash them

What did the Lord do on the third day (v. 11)?

came down on Mount Sinai

In verses 12–13, God instructed Moses to establish boundaries around the base of the mountain so the people would not touch it and be killed. Why do you think they would die, just for touching the mountain? It was God's will

In verse 14, Moses sanctified the people and had them wash their clothing. What does it mean to be sanctified? To cleasn to make Holy

Why do you believe the Lord instructed the men not to come near their wives (v. 15)? To Think of God only

Read verse 16 and fill in the blanks below describing how God made His entrance.

Then it came to pass on the ___3ed___ day, in the ___MOURNiNg___ that there were ___Thunder___ and ___Lighting___, and a thick ___Cloud___ on the mountain; and the ___loud___ of the ___tRumpEt___ was very loud, so that all the ___PEopl[e]___ who were in the camp ___tREmbLed___. *(Exod. 19:16 NKJV)*

Where did the people of Israel meet God (v. 17)? the foot of the mountain

In what did the Lord descend? In what was Mount Sinai completely covered (v. 18)? FiRE   Smoke

What was the message of warning the Lord gave Moses to deliver to the people (vv. 21–22)? Do not bREAk thRough oR thEy would DiE.

Read the remaining verses of this chapter. In your own words, tell why you believe Moses and Aaron were permitted to approach the Lord, while the others were not. They wERE his MESSAgE mERs

EXODUS 20

THE TEN COMMANDMENTS

The Ten Commandments have been celebrated throughout history as the fundamental expression of God's expectations for humankind. For centuries, they have been the measuring stick by which the children of Israel—and thus all others, as well—could know where they stood by knowing what God required of them.

But God didn't give the Ten Commandments so that people could attain righteousness by observing them. Righteousness before God can be attained only through faith in God. Rather, He gave the Ten Commandments to reveal to the Israelites— and thus to us, as well—their own sinfulness in contrast to His righteous standards. (This, incidentally, is what Paul means later on when he speaks of being "condemned by the law.")

Read verses 1 through 17, then write out the Ten Commandments as you would extract them directly from Scripture. When you are finished, compare your version with the chart on the following page showing the slight variations among the Jewish, Catholic, and Protestant versions.

1. you shall have no other Gods

2. you shall not make any idol or likeness what is in heaven

3. you shall not worship them

4. you shall not take the Lord name in vain

5. Honor your mother + father

6. you shall not murder

7. you shall not commit adultrey

8. you shall not steal

9. shall not bear false witness asinust you neighbor

10. Not covet neighboor's - wife + servents animal or anything

Verses 18–26 conclude this chapter by showing us how the children of Israel reacted to God's presence on the mountain. They were filled with fear and awe—to such an extent, in fact, that they asked to hear God speak *only through Moses!*

What were the people afraid would happen if they heard the Lord speak directly to them (v. 19)? Lest we die

Why is it good to have a healthy fear of God (v. 20)?
So you will not sin

What instructions did the Lord then give to the children of Israel (v. 23)? you shall ~~make~~ not make other gods besides me

Read verses 24–26, then explain what you believe God's require-ments with respect to altars and sacrifices revealed about Himself. Consider, also, what you know about other civilizations of that era and how they worshiped their own false gods. What do you think the Lord might have been trying to avoid?

HE WANTED it of SimpLE·fEARthLy MATERaL Nothing fANcEy

EXODUS 21

In chapters 21–23 of Exodus, God gave the children of Israel a series of statutes concerning issues of great importance to them in their daily lives. Clearly, He wanted to get them started "on the right foot" in their existence as a unique and separate nation, devoted entirely to Him. Read these three chapters and answer the questions that follow to become familiar with some of the Lord's most basic provisions for His own people in that era.

THE TREATMENT OF SERVANTS

Why do you think Hebrews were allowed to buy other Hebrews (v. 2)? I don't know it MAKES No SENSE

How many years did a servant need to work before his debt could be forgiven (v. 2)? 6 yR3

In verses 3–11 the Lord laid down some very specific instructions with respect to slaves and their families. Many of these condi-tions are difficult for us to comprehend here in the modern world. On the other hand, (1) do you think these verses were talking about people who were truly slaves, or about indentured servants? (2) What is the difference? And also, (3) what do you think of the difference between the rules dealing with female and

THE TEN COMMANDMENTS

The Ten Commandments have taken different forms down through the centuries, depending on who was interpreting the Scriptures. The Jewish version pre-dates all others, of course; the Catholic version came about in the fourth century AD, and the Protestant version came into being more than one thousand years later. The wording of each version might change depending on which translation of the Bible is being used, but these examples show the minor differences in the three major breakdowns of essentially the same biblical material—Exodus 20:1–17.

	Jewish[1]	Catholic[2]	Protestant[3]
I	I am the LORD your God who has taken you out of the land of Egypt.	I, the LORD, am your God. You shall not have other gods besides Me.	You shall have no other gods before Me.
II	You shall have no other gods but Me.	You shall not take the name of the LORD, your God, in vain.	You shall not make for yourself a carved image.
III	You shall not take the name of the LORD your God in vain.	Remember to keep holy the Sabbath day.	You shall not take the name of the LORD your God in vain.
IV	You shall remember the Sabbath and keep it holy.	Honor your father and your mother.	Remember the Sabbath day, to keep it holy.
V	Honor your mother and your father.	You shall not kill.	Honor your father and your mother.
VI	You shall not murder.	You shall not commit adultery.	You shall not murder.
VII	You shall not commit adultery.	You shall not steal.	You shall not commit adultery.
VIII	You shall not steal.	You shall not bear false witness.	You shall not steal.
IX	You shall not bear false witness.	You shall not covet your neighbor's wife.	You shall not bear false witness against your neighbor.
X	You shall not covet anything that belongs to your neighbor.	You shall not covet your neighbor's goods.	You shall not covet anything that is your neighbor's.

[1]Based on *Tanakh: The Holy Scriptures;* The New JPS Translation According to the Traditional Hebrew Text.
[2]Based on the New American Bible.
[3]Based on the New King James Version.

male slaves? Why were their "conditions of service" not always
identical? Discuss these questions in the numbered spaces.

1. YES truly SLAVES

2. if they had A wife And childreN
AFTER they were pAid for the MASTER
3. would keep them
The work would BE diFFerent
lighter + heavier

LAWS CONCERNING VIOLENCE

Under what circumstances did the Lord condone putting someone to death (vv. 12–17)? if he did Not Lie
iN wAit - or it wAs AcctedentAl

Fill in the blanks of verses 23 through 25 to reveal several familiar expressions.

But if any further injury follows, then you shall give
Life for life, eye for eye , tooth
for tooth , hand for hand, foot for foot,
burn for burn , wound for wound, stripe
for stripe. (Exod. 21:23–25 NKJV)

What did the Lord say should happen to the owner of an ox that
shows violent tendencies when that owner doesn't do anything to
control his ox (v. 29)? More important, what is the "general rule"
God is undoubtedly illustrating here?

EXODUS 22

RESPONSIBILITY FOR PROPERTY

According to verse 2, is it wrong to kill a thief if he breaks into
your home? ?

What are the instructions for a man whose animal causes damage to another's field or vineyard (v. 5)? HE MUST GiVE the bEST oF HiS fiELD oR ViNEYARd AS PAYMENT foR dAMAGES

What happens if a fire destroys someone's field or grain? HE who SEt thE fiRE MuST PAY UP

Verses 9–13 deal with several things that could happen between neighbors, between borrowers and lenders, and between those who hire others (or their animals) to work for them. In your own words, what are the general principles that seem to apply here? What mishaps, in general, is a man (or the owner of an animal) responsible for, and which ones is he not responsible for? if you boRRoW ANd it is RuiNEd you PAy uP. if you hiRE thE woRk doNE ANd it diES oR bREAkS ANd thE OWNER is thERE NO

MORAL AND CEREMONIAL PRINCIPLES ExtRA chARgE

Why should a man pay a bride-price for a seduction (vv. 16–17)? (Hint: How important was the virginity of his wife to a husband in that era?) if hE LiEs with A viRgiN thAt is NoT ENgAgEd. VERy

According to verses 18–20, what three kinds of people were permitted to live during these times? thosE who do Not sLEEp with ANiMAL, thosE who SAcRificE to God ANd thosE who ARE NoT SoRCERESSES

In your own words, why do you believe God refused to tolerate such "lifestyles"? thEy wERE sinful

Why do you think the Lord forbade the Israelites to charge interest when lending money to the poor—wouldn't that be an example of a double standard? ?

EXODUS 23

JUSTICE FOR ALL

According to verse 2, whom should you not follow—and for what purpose? A ~~MURit~~ MULtitudE

What were you to do if you saw your enemy's ox or donkey going astray (v. 4)? REtuRN it to him

Verses 1 through 9 discuss the laws of justice and mercy. In your own words, what was God's ultimate message here? BE hoNESt do No wRoNgfuL hELpiNg

THE LAW OF SABBATHS

When God decreed that the land should lie fallow every seventh year, He was doing at least three things: First, He was teaching the Israelites to trust Him for all their needs, without reservation. Second, He was teaching them not to be type-A personalities all the time; to "back off" from excessive work on a regular basis and allow themselves regular periods of rest and rejuvenation. And third, He was making sure the land got a chance to recover from heavy use, to replenish the nutrients and minerals He put there in the first place.

What were the Israelites instructed to do for food during the seventh year (vv. 10–11)? ThE 6th yEAR gAthEE ALL thE yEiLd. ANd LEt thE LANd REst thE 7th yEAR

What did God say that everyone should do on the seventh day (v. 12)? CEASE from LabOR ALL ANIMALS & SLAVES.

In conjunction with the above, God also mentioned three of the seven annual feasts (or festivals) that He ordained for His people, about which He went into considerable detail in Leviticus 23.

What three feasts did God require the children of Israel to observe (vv. 14–16)? FEAST of UNLEAVENED BREAD the FEAST of HARVEST - the FEAST of GatHERING

THE ANGEL AND THE PROMISES

Why did the Lord send the people an Angel (v. 20)?

to gUARd thEM ALONG the WAy

What did the Lord agree to do for the people if they obeyed the Angel (v. 22)? to bE A ENEMY to thEiR ENEMiES & A AdvERSARY to thEiR AdvERSARiES

What did the Lord promise to do for His people if they would serve Him properly (vv. 25–26)? DEstORY thE AMORiTES, HiTTiTES, PERiZZiTES, CANAANiTES, HivitES & JEbusitiES

Read verses 27–33, then explain why God wanted His people to take over the land He had designated for them in "small steps" rather than all at once. So thEy couLd thE LANd LittLE by LittLE

EXODUS 24

In this chapter, Israel affirms the basic stipulations of the covenant God had just established with them. These included the Ten Commandments plus all the other ordinances God had given them thus far.

The first eight verses describe how Moses prepared the people by building an altar at the foot of Mount Sinai, then erecting stone pillars to symbolize the twelve tribes of Israel.

From what book did Moses read (v. 7)?

the book of the covenant

What did Moses do to bind the covenant between the Lord and the people (v. 8)?

young bulls blood on sprinkled the people

What was under God's feet (v. 10)?

Appeared to be a pavement of sapphire, as clear as the sky

What tablets of stone was the Lord talking about (v. 12)?

with the law and the commandmen

How many days did Moses remain on the mountain (v. 18)?

for 40 days + 40 nights

The seven chapters of Exodus that complete this section (i.e., chapters 25–31) contain the remainder of what God said to Moses on Mount Sinai, concentrating on how the children of Israel were to worship Him from that day forward. The sub-headings that follow identify each of the major subjects covered in these chapters. Please read the chapters one by one and answer the following questions.

Exodus 25

Offerings for the Sanctuary

The Lord agreed to accept offerings from the children of Israel of very specific items, for very specific purposes (vv. 1–9). What were the items He was willing to accept? Also, where do you think the children of Israel got these items? gold, silver & bronze, blue purple and scarlet material fine linen, and goat hair. Rams skin dyed red porpoises kin acacia wood, oil for lighting spices for anointing oil for the fragrant incense,

The Ark of the Testimony onyx stones and setting stones

For what was the ark built (vv. 10–16)? made of acacia wood and gold and the testimony was to be placed inside

What two angelic beings were positioned to "cover" the mercy seat on the ark (v. 18)? cherubim

Where did God say He would meet with Moses (i.e., "from above" where?)? Above the mercy seat between the 2 cherbims

The Table for the Showbread

How would you characterize the general "look" of the table for the showbread (vv. 23–30)? fAbuLus of goLd And AcAciA wood

Why did God want it to be built—that is, how would it be used? to pouR LibAtions And sEt thē bREAd of thē PRESĒNCE ON thē tAbLē bēfoRE ME At ALL tiMES

The Golden Lampstand

What item was to be made all of one piece and from pure gold (v. 31)? Thē LAMp sthnd, shAft & BASE, it cups, buLBs And floWERS bRANches

How many branches were to come out of its sides (v. 32)? 6

How much gold did the Lord say should be used for this item? What would be the modern equivalent in terms of weight? Can you then calculate its "melt value" (i.e., the value of the pure metal all by itself) at current prices? (Note: This, of course, would not take into account its artistic or archaeological value! If the original menorah were to be found, its "market value" would be beyond calculation.)

This particular item has long been recognized as the national symbol for the State of Israel; it is used on their coins and in other places, as well. What is its common name?

tALēnt 75 lbz

EXODUS 26

THE TABERNACLE

How many curtains did God instruct Moses to make for the tabernacle (v. 1)?

How many loops did God say should be built into each curtain (v. 5)?

Of what were the curtains to be made?

Of what two skins was the tabernacle covering to be made (v. 14)?

How many sockets of silver were to be under the twenty boards?

Of what was the veil to be made (v. 31)?

What would be housed behind the veil?

What would the veil be (v. 33)? In other words, what was its official function?

Of what was the screen to be made (vv. 36–37)?

EXODUS 27

THE ALTAR OF THE BURNT OFFERING

In what shape was the altar to be made (v. 1)?

What kind of wood was to be used? (Note: Don't miss the sidebar in this chapter dealing with this particular choice of material!)

What were the people instructed to put on the four corners of the altar (v. 2)? What do you believe their purpose would be?

Of what were the utensils for use on the altar to be made (v. 3)?

THE COURT OF THE TABERNACLE

Considering all the dimensions given in verses 9–19, and knowing that a cubit is equal to about eighteen inches, what were the approximate dimensions of the outer wall of the tabernacle? What was the ratio of its length to its width? How high was it? Could the average man, standing next to the wall, see over the top?

THE CARE OF THE LAMPSTAND

What did God say should be used as fuel in the golden lampstand (v. 20)?

Why was the lamp to burn continually, and who was commissioned to attend to it?

EXODUS 28

GARMENTS FOR THE PRIESTHOOD

Whom did God commission to minister as priests before Him (v. 1)?

For what two reasons were Aaron's holy garments to be made (v. 2)?

With what did God fill all the artisans (v. 3)?

What were the six garments they were to make for Aaron (v. 4)?

THE EPHOD

What colors was the ephod to be (v. 5)?

What was to be engraved on the two onyx stones (v. 9)?

Where were the two stones to be placed on the ephod (v. 12)?

THE BREASTPLATE

What is the breastplate called in verse 15?

What twelve stones were to be placed in the breastplate (vv. 17–20)?

OTHER PRIESTLY GARMENTS

In what color was the robe to be made (v. 31)?

What was to be sewn on its hem (v. 33)?

What was engraved on the gold plate (v. 36)?

Where was the plate to be positioned on Aaron's body, and why?

Besides Aaron, who else would be consecrated to minister before the Lord (v. 41)?

EXODUS 29

HOW THE SACRIFICES WERE MADE

What would be on Aaron's head when he was anointed (v. 7)?

DOES GOD APPRECIATE BEAUTY?

Many different Christian organizations down through the centuries have argued that God appreciates plainness above all else. They have sometimes tried to give it to Him to the point of austerity in building design, furniture, and clothing.

On the other hand, although almost no one would argue that God does not appreciate simplicity of design (what could be simpler—yet more functional—than a lamp with seven hollow branches arising from a central pool of oil, all to be lit at once?), the idea that God does not appreciate beauty for its own sake seems foreign to other people. Why else would He design and create such gorgeous flowers, towering mountains, shimmering lakes, and resplendent rainbows?

Another indicator must certainly be the Israelite tabernacle and its artifacts, as designed by God for the Israelites' worship of Him in an utterly barren wilderness. Or the magnificent temple He eventually commissioned Solomon to build, replete with gold leaf on the walls and ornamentation on all the columns.

Does this mean that congregations should spend significant portions of their income on impressive buildings and expensive implements of worship? Certainly not! We can surmise that God enjoys beauty, but we need not assume that He requires us to create it for Him as a condition of His favor. Beauty of heart would certainly be more important to Him, as revealed in the purity of our thoughts, motives, and actions.

Thus the woman who poured the perfume over Christ's feet pleased Him because she did so out of purest love. Yet God did not *demand* that action. As with all such considerations, God is above all a God of order—of *balance*. Wild extravagance can coexist with stark simplicity—either one can even enhance the other. The trick is not to insist on one extreme all the time.

Where were Aaron and his sons to put their hands before they sacrificed the bull (v. 10)?

What part of the bull was to be burned with fire outside the camp (v. 14)?

What kind of offering was this?

What part of the ram was to be burned on the altar (v. 18)?

What kind of offering was this?

What type of offering is described in verses 22–25?

Where were the flesh and bread to be eaten (v. 32)?

What would happen to the flesh if it was left overnight?

For how many days would Aaron and his sons be required to go through the consecration process (v. 35)?

THE DAILY OFFERINGS

What was the continual offering the people were to make (vv. 38–42)?

WHAT WERE THE URIM AND THE THUMMIN?

Down through the centuries, many people have asked how the
Urim and the Thummin worked. That is, how were they used by the head priest to
get answers from God? Also, would not the use of such obviously mechanical
methods be an example of forbidden divination?

The answer to the first question is that no one really knows how they were
shaped or used. We know they were objects that fit into a pouch of the breastplate
worn by the high priest, to whom their use was restricted by God. But we simply
do not know how God used them to respond to questions from the priest.

With respect to divination, the obvious answer is that God established the use
of the Urim and the Thummin Himself. The answers they gave had the same
authority as any other form of divine revelation and were always absolutely true.
Thus we really can't compare this with other forms of divination, as established by
humans, to worship or seek the counsel of false gods.

*Where would the Lord meet the people to speak with them
(v. 42)?*

How was the tabernacle to be sanctified (v. 43)?

*Fill in the blanks below to see what God promised the children of
Israel.*

*"I will dwell _____ the children of Israel and will
be their _____. And they shall know that I am
the _____ their God, who brought them up out of
the land of _____, that I may _____
among them. I am the LORD their God." (Exod.
29:45–46 NKJV)*

Exodus 30

The Altar of Incense

What was to be burned on the altar (v. 1)?

Read verses 9–10 and explain why the people were instructed not to burn any offering on this altar other than sweet incense.

The Ransom Money

How much money was each person to give during the census (v. 13)?

What was the minimum age at which this offering would be required?

How would this offering be used, according to verse 16?

The Bronze Laver

What was the laver of bronze to be used for (v. 18)?

What would happen to those who offered a burnt offering without first washing their hands and feet (vv. 19–20)?

THE HOLY ANOINTING OIL

What were the five ingredients the Lord instructed Moses to use to make the anointing oil (vv. 22–25)?

What was to be anointed with the oil (vv. 26–28)?

What would cause a person to be cut off from his people (v. 33)?

WHY DID GOD SPECIFY ACACIA WOOD?

Acacia wood comes from a tree (also known as the Shittah tree) that grows remarkably well all over the deserts of Sinai and the area around the Dead Sea, sometimes attaining a height of twenty feet or more. The wood itself is very hard and very heavy, with a beautiful grain that is generally brownish-orange in color.

Acacia wood also features two characteristics that would make it ideal for the Ark of the Covenant and other wood-based furniture and fittings for the tabernacle: (1) It is impervious to insects and is thus nearly incorruptible by ordinary means, and (2) it displays an unusual property known as *chatoyancy,* meaning that it appears to change colors and luster under different lighting conditions. Thus it would be especially beautiful—and constantly "new"—in the flickering light of the menorah within the inner courtyard of the tabernacle.

THE INCENSE

What spices did the Lord instruct Moses to use to make incense (vv. 34–35)?

What was the sole purpose of this incense (v. 27)?

Exodus 31

In what ways was Bezalel filled with the Spirit of God (vv. 3–5)?

The Sabbath Law

How was the Sabbath a sign (vv. 12–17)?

What would be the consequence for working on the Sabbath?

What was the Sabbath called (v. 16)?

When God finished speaking with Moses, how did He write on the tablets of stone (v. 18)?

PULLING IT ALL TOGETHER . . .

• God called Moses to the top of Mount Sinai, where He gave
him the Ten Commandments.

• God also gave Moses a series of instructions explaining how
the children of Israel were to worship Him from that day forward. In particular, He instructed them in . . .

  • how they were to treat each other;
  • how they were to treat their animals and take
    responsibility for their animals' conduct;
  • how they were to prepare the tabernacle, its furnish-
    ings, the Ark of the Covenant, the priestly garments,
    and all the accessories with which they would wor-
    ship Him; and
  • how the priests were to perform the sacrifices.

• God instructed Moses to present these aspects of His
covenant with His people, and the people agreed to be
bound by God's commandments.

6 FAILURE AND RESTORATION

EXODUS 32:1–34:35

Before We Begin . . .

Almost everyone knows that Moses reacted rather strongly to the children of Israel's conduct while he was on Mount Sinai receiving the Ten Commandments. What is your personal feeling about what he did when he came down the mountain and saw what was going on?

Moses was more than a little forward in some of his conversations with God. Do you think some of his boldness was justified? If so, how and why? Do you believe the will of an individual should be capable of changing the mind of God?

The whining, the griping, the pettiness, and the many small failures of the children of Israel have been recorded in the first thirty-one chapters of Exodus, leading up to this moment. In other words, the basic human failings graphically demonstrating the vast difference between themselves and God have been on clear display.

But what's hard to deny, in the opinion of many scholars, is that the children of Israel did what many of us would have done today in similar circumstances. So let us not judge them ourselves. Let us marvel instead at the means by which the Lord, despite His anger, managed to deal with their failures and restore them to His favor. Incidentally, this same pattern of failure and restoration would repeat itself over and over throughout the long history of God's chosen people, until He finally punished them once again, more than a thousand years later, by allowing them to fall back into another four centuries of slavery, this time at the hands of the Babylonians and Assyrians. But even this was not final, for God again brought them back and restored them in the eyes of the world to the position they have occupied since God first promised Abraham to make of his descendants a great nation.

Meanwhile, here in the last third of the book of Exodus, it is almost impossible to read the conversations between God and Moses without being profoundly affected. Surely God knew what He was doing when He raised up Moses to his leadership position. Listen to the man speak in the verses ahead! Perhaps no person in history has ever spoken so clearly and often so convincingly to the Lord Himself, even when they disagreed. Nor has anyone ever been so honored and respected by God— not only as a friend, but as a true *covenant partner* in the vast undertaking they shared together.

That undertaking, of course, was the job of turning a huge, frightened, fresh-from-captivity rabble into a powerful nation willing to trust God to direct their affairs. They didn't always trust Him in the beginning, did they? Nor have they always done so in the years since then.

But one thing has always remained true and unchanging, and that is the covenant God established with them, to love and protect them forever.

Please begin this portion of our study by reading Exodus 32 and answering the following questions.

EXODUS 32

THE GOLDEN CALF

What did the people ask Aaron to do when Moses didn't come back from Mount Sinai right away (v. 1)?

What mistake did Aaron make (vv. 2–4)?

What did the Lord call the children of Israel (v. 7)?

What did the Lord say to Moses about the children of Israel (vv. 8–10)? To get the whole story, fill in the blanks in the passage below:

> "I have seen this people, and indeed it is a _____
> _____! Now therefore, let Me alone, that My _____
> may _____ _____ against them and I may _____
> them. And I will make of you a _____ _____."
> (Exod. 32:9–10 NKJV)

What do you think—was God really serious when He threatened to destroy His people?

Of what promise did Moses remind the Lord (v. 13)?

In your own words, answer this question: Does the Lord ever change His mind? If so, what might be one obvious cause?

What did Moses bring down the mountain with him (v. 15)?

Whose writing was on the tablets?

What noise did Joshua hear in the camp (v. 18)?

What caused Moses to become angry? As a result, what happened to the tablets?

WHAT DOES IT MEAN TO BE STIFF-NECKED?

The children of Israel are called "stiff-necked" about a dozen times in the Bible, both by God and by others. What does this expression mean?

The farmers of biblical times plowed their fields and did other demanding work with oxen, fashioning heavy wooden yokes that fit around the animals' necks and rested against their powerful shoulders. The yokes were then attached to wagons, plows, or other implements, which the oxen pulled by walking forward and pushing against the wooden yokes.

Whenever a farmer wanted to train a young ox to work the fields, he would place the ox in a double-yoke beside an older, experienced ox so the youngster could learn from his elder. However, every once in a while the children of Israel would encounter a young ox who simply refused to lower his head so the yoke could be fastened around his neck.

He was too stiff-necked, and thus the same expression came to refer to anyone who refused to submit to authority, especially that of God.

What were the four things Moses did to the golden calf (v. 20)?

1.

2.

3.

4.

Why did Moses blame Aaron for the people's sin? Do you consider that fair?

Who came to Moses when called (v. 26)?

What did Moses command the sons of Levi to do (vv. 27–28)? Why would he call on the Levites to do this? And most important of all, on whose authority do you believe Moses would do such a thing?

How many people died that day?

What did Moses ask of the Lord (vv. 30–32)?

Whom did the Lord say He would blot out of His book (v. 33)?

Whom did the Lord say would go before Moses and the people (v. 34)?

Finally, as this chapter ends, what was the Lord's attitude toward His people? Had He forgiven them for worshiping their golden calf? Did that mean they would no longer be punished?

EXODUS 33

By the time chapter 33 begins, many of those who instigated the golden calf affair had already been put to death, at God's command, by the Levites. Moses had then prayed for atonement for the rest of the people (for thousands had participated), and God had promised to punish the remaining guilty ones in other ways.

Now, after the Israelites' months-long encampment at Mount Sinai, God told Moses that he and the people should again proceed toward the Promised Land but that God Himself would no longer travel with them. Instead, He would send His Angel to lead them, but He would not travel in their midst anymore for fear that He might be further inclined to destroy them along the way.

This Moses could not accept, and thus we see the results of the continuing interchange between God and Moses as the chapter unfolds.

MOSES MEETS WITH THE LORD

Read verses 1–6 and explain why the people were mourning.

In your own words, explain what the tabernacle of meeting (sometimes called the tent of meeting in other translations) was, as described in verses 7–11. What went on there? What happened whenever Moses entered?

What do you think it means to speak "face-to-face" with the Lord, as we are told Moses did (v. 11)? Does this mean that Moses was able to see the Lord's actual form and face?

Who stayed behind at the tabernacle whenever Moses left (v. 11)? Do you recognize this person's name?

THE PROMISE OF GOD'S PRESENCE

In verse 13, Moses used an expression that occurs fairly often in the Old Testament: "if I have found grace [or favor] in Your sight." What does this phrase mean?

What did God say He would do for Moses and His people (v. 14)?

Read verse 16 carefully, then explain why Moses was concerned that Israel should be distinct (i.e., "separate") from other nations. In what way? Why would this be so important to Moses?

What did Moses ask God if he could see (v. 18)?

What did God say would happen if Moses saw His face?

How did God agree to cover Moses as he stood in the cleft of the rock while He passed by?

What would Moses see after the Lord took away the covering?

EXODUS 34

HOW THE LAW WAS RECORDED

Exodus 34 recounts what happened when Moses went back up onto Mount Sinai to undo the destruction of the tablets containing the Ten Commandments. Read the entire chapter and answer the questions below.

Who promised to write His commandments on the new set of tablets, cut from stone by Moses (v. 1)?

Why would the Lord replace the tablets that Moses broke?

Verses 6–7 reveal what many scholars call the attributes of God, as given to us in His own words. Read these two verses and fill in the blanks below. Then list, in the blank space below the passage, as many of God's attributes as you can identify from the text. Finally, read the sidebar entitled "What Are the Attributes of God?" on page 116 to see how close you came to getting all thirteen.

> And the LORD _____ before him and _____, "The LORD, the LORD God, _____ and _____, _____, and abounding in _____ and _____, keeping mercy for thousands, forgiving iniquity and _____ and sin, by no means _____ the guilty, visiting the iniquity of the _____ upon the children and the children's children to the third and the fourth _____."

Why do you think the Lord indulged Moses' request in such a dramatic way?

How did Moses show reverence and thankfulness for the Lord's revelation of Himself?

Do you think it's possible today to have the same close relationship with the Lord that Moses had?

In what ways do you feel the Lord reveals His character to you personally?

WHAT ARE THE ATTRIBUTES OF GOD?

Exodus 34:6–7 lists up to thirteen attributes of God, as revealed in His own words to Moses. We say "up to" because different scholars compose the list in different ways. Here is one of the more traditional listings emerging from these verses:

1. The same before and after a person sins
2. God, the almighty Lord of the universe
3. Merciful
4. Gracious
5. Long-suffering
6. Abundant in goodness
7. Abundant in truth
8. Keeping mercy unto the thousandth generation
9. Forgiving iniquity
10. Forgiving transgression
11. Forgiving sin
12. Will by no means clear the guilty
13. Visiting the iniquity of the fathers unto the fourth generation.

THE COVENANT RENEWED

What did the Lord promise to do (v. 10)?

What did the Lord command the Israelites not to do (v. 12)?

What things did He command them to destroy (v. 13)? Why? What did they represent?

What specific instructions did the Lord give His people about the inhabitants of the lands they were about to enter?

What instructions did the Lord give—again—about the work week, the Sabbath, and the feasts that He wanted them to observe?

How many days and nights did Moses fast with the Lord this time (v. 28)?

What was different about Moses when he came down from the mountain?

What do you think caused this physical change?

Why did Moses cover his face each time he finished speaking with the people? Why would he uncover it when he went into the tent of meeting to speak with God?

PULLING IT ALL TOGETHER . . .

• God commanded Moses to return to the top of Mount Sinai, bringing a fresh set of blank stone tablets with him.

• Moses did as he was ordered, but he also asked God for the privilege of actually seeing Him.

• God allowed Moses to stand in a cleft of rock, covered Moses' face with His own hand while He passed by, then allowed Moses to see Him from the back.

• God described Himself in Exodus 34, giving us what many call the thirteen-point list of God's attributes.

• God wrote the Ten Commandments on the new tablets, then gave Moses another forty days and forty nights of additional conversation and instructions as to how the Israelites were to worship Him.

7 WILDERNESS WORSHIP

EXODUS 35:1–40:38

Before We Begin ...

What is your concept of the wilderness tabernacle? What kind of a building was it, anyway? What would it most look like today?

Why do you think God was so concerned with having the children of Israel build His tabernacle and all its accessories to such rigid, detailed specifications? Why did the details seem to matter so much to Him?

The last six chapters of Exodus contain a certain amount of near-duplication, for much of this material is quite similar to God's instructions as recorded by Moses in chapters 25–31. This is especially true of the material dealing with the building of the tabernacle and the making of the furniture, the articles of worship, and the priestly garments. The chief difference lies in the tense Moses used when writing these sections—mostly present tense in the earlier chapters; mostly past tense in the later ones.

For that reason alone, the later chapters seem more definitive, for they speak of *what was actually done* rather than what was yet to do. They also reveal at least two reasons why God might have given what seems like repetition at first glance but really isn't.

1. First, He undoubtedly wanted to make it very clear that He is a faithful God who works with His people in spite of their failures. He even agreed to continue dwelling among them after they rejected Him in favor of the golden calf back at Mount Sinai.

2. Second, He probably wanted to emphasize the obedience of Moses, who did exactly as God commanded him to do, over and over again, even when it must have seemed like he was the only person in the entire nation of Israel willing to remain faithful to God. Several other Scriptures in various parts of the Bible emphasize this point independently—that Moses, often called the greatest leader the children of Israel ever had, above all else was faithful to God even as God was faithful to His people.

With all that in mind, please read Exodus 35 and answer the following questions—which we hope will not seem like repetition of the questions you have answered so far!

EXODUS 35

What did the Lord say would happen to those who worked on the Sabbath (v. 2)?

Would the Israelites be allowed to kindle a fire on the Sabbath (v. 3)?

WHAT HAPPENED TO THE ARK?

As anyone who has seen the movie *Raiders of the Lost Ark* can attest, millions of people would like to know what actually happened to the Ark of the Covenant—and where it has been kept all these years. Many different theories have been put forth down through the centuries. For example . . .

Some say it's buried somewhere on the west bank of the Jordan, near where the Dead Sea Scrolls were found about sixty years ago—perhaps in one of the caves used by the Qumran community, which included John the Baptist.

Some say that it's more likely to be on Mount Nebo on the east bank of the Jordan, in the modern nation of Jordan.

Some say it's buried somewhere under Jerusalem. Popular suggestions include (1) the site of the actual crucifixion, (2) the Temple Mount, or (3) a secret tunnel carved in stone, somewhere under the city.

Finally, one of the more popular stories suggests that the Ark was taken from Jerusalem in the days of King Solomon, by a son born to Solomon and the Queen of Sheba. This son supposedly took the Ark back to Sheba (now thought to be modern Ethiopia) for safekeeping, and it has remained hidden there for hundreds of years.

Surely time will tell . . .

OFFERINGS FOR THE TABERNACLE

What kind of heart did the Israelites need to have before they could bring an offering to the Lord (v. 5)?

List the three precious metals acceptable as an offering (v. 5)?

What color were the ram skins God wanted (v. 7)?

What stones were acceptable for an offering, and where were they to be set?

ARTICLES OF THE TABERNACLE

According to verses 10–19, what were the five major pieces of furniture to be built for the tabernacle? List each one, but include only the five main items themselves—not their accessories.

1.

2.

3.

4.

5.

THE TABERNACLE OFFERINGS PRESENTED

Who came to contribute to the Lord's offering (v. 21)?

What type of jewelry was offered (v. 22)?

Who spun yarn as an offering (v. 25)?

What is the meaning of the phrase "the women whose hearts stirred with wisdom" (v. 26)?

Who brought onyx stones to be set in the ephod and the breast-plate?

EXODUS 36

THE ARTISANS CALLED BY GOD

The story of Aholiab and Bezalel—and especially Bezalel because he is mentioned several times—is particularly inspiring. The story actually starts with Exodus 35:30 and continues through 36:2.

Exodus 35:34 tells us that God put the ability to teach into the hearts of both Bezalel and Aholiab. Thus not only were they the two men most responsible for creating the beautiful articles of worship God required for the tabernacle, but they also were the ones who taught many others to do the same kinds of things. They worked with the most rudimentary of materials, with nothing but their bare hands and whatever tools they brought with them from Egypt or were able to fashion in the wilderness. However, their work was enhanced by God's limitless knowledge of metallurgy, carpentry, gem and stonecutting, masonry, and all the other skills they required—not to mention engraving, designing, and tapestry making as mentioned in Exodus 35:35.

We have already mentioned Bezalel's work on the menorah—but think again of the difficulty of fabricating that hollow-stemmed, seven-branch masterpiece by hammering it out of one lump of solid gold!

Now read through Exodus 36 and answer the following questions, knowing that the word *he* most likely applies to Bezalel as the overseer of most of the work.

What time of the day were offerings brought (v. 3)?

Did the offerings supply enough material to build the tabernacle according to the Lord's instruction?

Why did the people give so freely?

And by the way—if the children of Israel were slaves in Egypt, where do you think they got so many precious items to give as offerings?

BUILDING THE TABERNACLE

What was the main embellishment the artisans added to the woven curtains (v. 8)?

What material did they use to make the curtains?

What two types of skin were used to make coverings for the tent (v. 19)? Why do you believe those two were chosen?

What type of wood was used on the tabernacle (v. 20)?

What precious metal was used over the acacia wood, and why was this metal chosen?

EXODUS 37

MAKING THE ARK OF THE TESTIMONY

Of what was the molding of the Ark made (v. 2)?

Of what were the poles that were used to carry the Ark made?

MAKING THE TABLE FOR THE SHOWBREAD

Of what were the utensils made (v. 16)?

List the utensils made for the table for the showbread (v. 16).

MAKING THE GOLD LAMPSTAND AND THE ALTAR OF INCENSE

We have already mentioned the gold lampstand (menorah) several times. Verses 17–24 give us several more details of its construction. In particular, with what kind of blossoms (fashioned of that huge original lump of gold, of course!) did God command Bezalel to decorate each of the seven branches?

Of what was the incense altar made (v. 25)?

In what shape was it made?

EXODUS 38

MAKING THE ALTAR OF BURNT OFFERING

The altar of burnt offering was overlaid with a different precious metal (v. 2). What was it?

List the five utensils made to accompany the altar (v. 3).

MAKING THE BRONZE LAVER

From where did the bronze for this item come (v. 8)?

MAKING THE COURT OF THE TABERNACLE

What metal was used on the court of the tabernacle?

MATERIALS OF THE TABERNACLE

Who made the tabernacle as the Lord had commanded (v. 22)?

What was the approximate weight of the gold, silver, and bronze used in the construction of the tabernacle (vv. 24–29)?

How much was a bekah worth (v. 26)?

EXODUS 39

Who wore the garments of ministry (v. 1)?

MAKING THE EPHOD

Why all the fancy clothing?

MAKING THE BREASTPLATE

In what shape was the breastplate made (v. 9)?

What stones were used in it (vv. 10–13)?

What was the significance of these stones (v. 14)?

MAKING THE OTHER PRIESTLY GARMENTS

What color was the robe of the ephod (v. 22)?

What fruit was woven onto the hem of the robe (v. 24)?

What color were the bells on the hem of the robe (v. 25)?

For whom were the tunics made (v. 27)?

What was the inscription on the holy crown (v. 30)?

Who was to wear the crown?

How was the crown fastened to the turban?

THE WORK COMPLETED

What did Moses do after he saw that the children of Israel had done everything as the Lord had commanded (v. 43)?

How did the Levites carry so many heavy objects?

EXODUS 40

Finally, all was in readiness, and the Lord commanded Moses to erect the tabernacle, clean all the accessories and position them in their proper places, and dedicate everything properly to the worship of Him.

THE TABERNACLE FINISHED

What was the significance of anointing all the objects?

Anointing Aaron's sons would ensure what (v. 15)?

How long had it been since the Israelites had left Egypt when the tabernacle was finished?

Who arranged all of the objects as the Lord had commanded him?

THE CLOUD AND THE GLORY

What filled the tabernacle (v. 34)?

Why couldn't Moses enter the tabernacle of meeting?

If Moses couldn't enter the tabernacle of meeting, who could?

What was the signal for the children of Israel to go onward in their journey?

What sign of the Lord was viewable by day, and what sign was viewable by night?

Why do you think the book of Exodus includes so many details— so many measurements and descriptions of materials? Why do you think God considered it important for these details to be included?

PULLING IT ALL TOGETHER . . .

• In these chapters, God gave Moses instructions—again—for how to build the tabernacle and all its accessories. This time, however, the work was actually completed.

• The tabernacle was erected for the first time and dedicated to the Lord on the first day of the new year. Thus began the second year of the children of Israel's freedom from slavery in Egypt.

• From that day forward, the cloud of the Lord covered the tabernacle when it was set up but lifted above it whenever it was time for the children of Israel to resume their travels.

8

COMING TO A CLOSE

It's no easy matter to draw the most meaningful conclusions from any book of the Bible in one thousand words or less. This is especially true if the goal is to find a central message that resonates with unmistakable clarity throughout that whole book. What, for example, might be the central, most distinct message of Exodus? Could it be . . .

1. That God kept His promise to Abraham, Isaac, and Jacob and thus carved His own nation out of Abraham's descendants?

2. That God loved His own people ahead of all others but also demanded much more from them in return?

3. That God, in fact, desired to use His chosen nation to teach others about Himself—literally, to bring full knowledge of His plan of salvation for all humankind to all the nations of the earth?

4. That Moses was perhaps the most faithful servant God had ever raised up, but even he could not keep the people he led from whining, grumbling, and failing God on numerous occasions?

5. That all people have resembled the children of Israel down through the centuries, with their faults and failings and yet their occasional moments of glory?

Obviously, any of the above would be correct, though none would be sufficient by itself. And perhaps more important, all of the above concentrate on the *history* contained in the book of Exodus, mingled with the portions that deal with the laws and guidelines for righteous conduct that make up much of the rest.

However, maybe there's a subtext, as well. And maybe, just maybe, it can be found in the way God dealt with His own people, linked to the way He tells us over and over, throughout His Word, that He would like to deal with each of us—individually—even today.

Oh sure, God is the One who rescues His own people from slavery. He is the One who calms the weather, commands the sun, and controls the seas. But He is also the One who brings His people their daily bread; who shows them what route to follow everywhere they go; who tells them what fabrics to use for the clothing their priests wear, and what color the decorative threads should be in the curtains they make for His tabernacle.

Thus our God is a God of almighty things, but He is also a God of details. This fact has been noted in dozens of books and thousands of sermons, but the book of Exodus has not always been used as an illustration. Nonetheless, the proof is in the text. Likewise, the only logical conclusion is in there, too.

God cares about everything. He cared enough about the children of Israel to take care of their daily needs for forty long years! He cared enough to tell them what was right and what was wrong, and even got ticked off when they didn't do what He'd told them—like any other parent worthy of the title would.

As with everything else about God, His love for us is in the small things, the things we might call insignificant if He didn't use them to show us that He cares.
The details. God is not remote, not impressed by His own sovereignty, not too busy sunning Himself in the heavens to care about every single detail in your life. Though they often made Him sad, He cared deeply about every single one of the people He led out of Egypt, and every single detail in each of their lives. And He cares just as much for you.

HOW TO BUILD YOUR REFERENCE LIBRARY

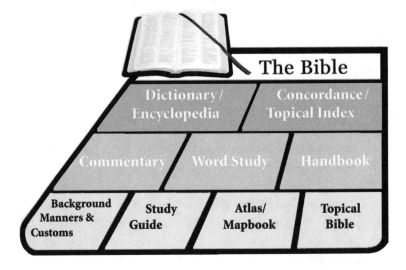

GREAT RESOURCES FOR BUILDING YOUR REFERENCE LIBRARY

DICTIONARIES AND ENCYCLOPEDIAS

All About the Bible: The Ultimate A-to-Z® Illustrated Guide to the Key People, Places, and Things

Every Man in the Bible by Larry Richards

Every Woman in the Bible by Larry Richards and Sue Richards

Nelson's Compact Bible Dictionary

Nelson's Illustrated Encyclopedia of the Bible

Nelson's New Illustrated Bible Dictionary

Nelson's Student Bible Dictionary

So That's What It Means! The Ultimate A-to-Z Resource by Don Campbell, Wendell Johnston, John Walvoord, and John Witmer

Vine's Complete Expository Dictionary of Old and New Testament Words by W. E. Vine and Merrill F. Unger

CONCORDANCES AND TOPICAL INDEXES

Nelson's Quick Reference Bible Concordance by Ronald F. Youngblood

The New Strong's Exhaustive Concordance of the Bible by James Strong

COMMENTARIES

Believer's Bible Commentary by William MacDonald

Matthew Henry's Concise Commentary on the Whole Bible by Matthew Henry

The MacArthur Bible Commentary by John MacArthur

Nelson's New Illustrated Bible Commentary

Thru the Bible series by J. Vernon McGee

HANDBOOKS

Nelson's Compact Bible Handbook

Nelson's Complete Book of Bible Maps and Charts

Nelson's Illustrated Bible Handbook

Nelson's New Illustrated Bible Manners and Customs by Howard F. Vos

With the Word: The Chapter-by-Chapter Bible Handbook by Warren W. Wiersbe

For more great resources, please visit *www.thomasnelson.com.*

NELSON IMPACT™ STUDY GUIDES

NELSON IMPACT

A Division of Thomas Nelson Publishers

Since 1798

The Nelson Impact Team is here to answer your questions
and suggestions as to how we can create more resources
that benefit you, your family, and your community.

Contact us at Impact@thomasnelson.com